Do it **The Lazy Way**

alpha books

1. To save steps, store a complete set of c_____ _____nk in each bathroom.

2. Put paper under your pet's food dish t_____

3. To eliminate messy cupboards filled haphazardly with pots and lids, store the cover on the pot to which it belongs.

4. Store extra plastic garbage bags right in the bottom of the garbage can. When the current bag is full, pull it out, tie it up, and then pull up the new clean bag.

5. Put dirty dishes directly into the dishwasher. Leaving them in the sink just makes the kitchen look dirty.

The Lazy Way
alpha books

*One luxurious
bubble bath*

The Lazy Way
alpha books

*Access to most comfortable
chair and favorite TV show*

The Lazy Way
alpha books

*One half-hour massage
(will need to recruit spouse, child, friend)*

The Lazy Way
alpha books

*Time to recline and listen to a favorite cd
(or at least one song)*

cut

6. You can get a lot of cleaning tasks done while talking on the phone.

7. Cleaning with paper towels eliminates having to wash the dust cloths.

8. As a reward, every once in a while let the kids sleep in their sleeping bags on top of their already-made beds. It will shorten your morning rush as well as theirs.

9. Don't put off until tomorrow what you can do now. A quick pick-up, rinse and put-it-away will save you scraping and scrubbing in the morning.

10. Don't clean something if it's not dirty.

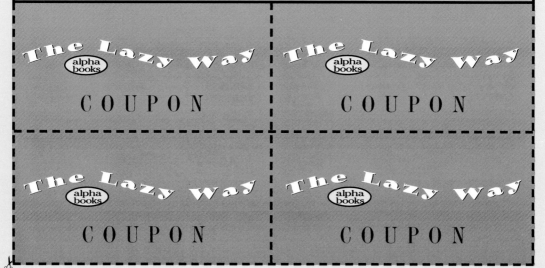

Clean
Your
House

Clean Your House

Barbara H. Durham

Macmillan • USA

Macmillan Publishing books may be purchased for business or sales promotional use. For information please write: Special Markets Department, Macmillan Publishing USA, 1633 Broadway, New York, NY 10019.

International Standard Book Number: 0-02-862649-4
Library of Congress Catalog Card Number: 98-88081

01   00   99   8   7   6   5   4   3   2   1

Interpretation of the printing code: the rightmost number of the first series of numbers is the year of the book's printing; the rightmost number of the second series of numbers is the number of the book's printing. For example, a printing code of 99-1 shows that the first printing occurred in 1999.

Printed in the United States of America

Page creation by Carrie Allen, Eric Brinkman, and Heather Pope.

You Don't Have to Feel Guilty Anymore!

IT'S O.K. TO DO IT *The Lazy Way*!

It seems every time we turn around, we're given more responsibility, more information to absorb, more places we need to go, and more numbers, dates, and names to remember. Both our bodies and our minds are already on overload. And we know what happens next—cleaning the house, balancing the checkbook, and cooking dinner get put off until "tomorrow" and eventually fall by the wayside.

So let's be frank—we're all starting to feel a bit guilty about the dirty laundry, stacks of ATM slips, and Chinese take-out. Just thinking about tackling those terrible tasks makes you exhausted, right? If only there were an easy, effortless way to get this stuff done! (And done right!)

There is—*The Lazy Way*! By providing the pain-free way to do something—including tons of shortcuts and time-saving tips, as well as lists of all the stuff you'll ever need to get it done efficiently—*The Lazy Way* series cuts through all of the time-wasting thought processes and laborious exercises. You'll discover the secrets of those who have figured out *The Lazy Way*. You'll get things done in half the time it takes the average person—and then you will sit back and smugly consider those poor suckers who haven't discovered *The Lazy Way* yet. With *The Lazy Way,* you'll learn how to put in minimal effort and get maximum results so you can devote your attention and energy to the pleasures in life!

v

The Lazy Way PROMISE

Everyone on *The Lazy Way* staff promises that, if you adopt *The Lazy Way* philosophy, you'll never break a sweat, you'll barely lift a finger, you won't put strain on your brain, and you'll have plenty of time to put up your feet. We guarantee you will find that these activities are no longer hardships, since you're doing them *The Lazy Way*. We also firmly support taking breaks and encourage rewarding yourself (we even offer our suggestions in each book!). With *The Lazy Way*, the only thing you'll be overwhelmed by is all of your newfound free time!

The Lazy Way SPECIAL FEATURES

Every book in our series features the following sidebars in the margins, all designed to save you time and aggravation down the road.

- **"Quick 'n Painless"**—shortcuts that get the job done fast.
- **"You'll Thank Yourself Later"**—advice that saves time down the road.
- **"A Complete Waste of Time"**—warnings that spare countless headaches and squandered hours.
- **"If You're So Inclined"**—optional tips for moments of inspired added effort.
- **"The Lazy Way"**—rewards to make the task more pleasurable.

If you've either decided to give up altogether or have taken a strong interest in the subject, you'll find information on hiring outside help with "How to Get Someone Else to Do It" as well as further reading recommendations in "If You Want to Learn More, Read These." In addition, there's an only-what-you-need-to-know glossary of terms and product names ("If You Don't Know What It Means/Does, Look Here") as well as "Lazy Rewards"—fun and relaxing ways to treat yourself for a job well done.

With *The Lazy Way* series, you'll find that getting the job done has never been so painless!

Series Editor
Amy Gordon

Cover Designer
Michael Freeland

Editorial Director
Gary Krebs

Managing Editor
Robert Shuman

Director of Creative Services
Michele Laseau

Production Editor
Robyn Burnett

What's in This Book

Housecleaning Is Not A Dirty Word

If your busy life doesn't leave you enough time for housecleaning but you can't stand looking at a sink full of dirty dishes, the dust on the tabletops, and the toothpaste globs on the bathroom counter, this book is for you. Think the only solution is to scrub and scour? No way! *Clean Your House The Lazy Way* will show you how to have a clean and tidy house you can be proud of, and still have time for all the other things you want to do.

Perhaps your day, like mine, begins at six in the morning with a quick workout before it's off to the office, then back home around seven. My husband and I are empty nesters with five adult children, three children-in-law, and, at this writing, two grandchildren. We know first hand what it's like to bundle kids off to day care and school, and not have enough time left to do anything for ourselves. Whether you spend your days at home with the kids or away at work, I bet cleaning house is the last thing you feel like doing when you get a little time to spare. But in the long run, a neat and organized home can be a port in the storm of your chaotic existence.

The tips in this book will take the sting out of housecleaning by showing you how to organize your supplies and tasks, and even eliminate some major cleaning jobs once you get into a regular maintenance routine. If you give your home a frequent once-over, whatever mess you face day to day is nothing in comparison to what you'd be looking at the end of a week if you didn't. It's much easier to use a paper towel than a chisel!

What you'll find in these chapters are strategies and shortcuts I use in my own home, and some that friends and associates have told me about. As I went about collecting hints from a variety of sources, I discovered that none of them were completely new. Several friends gave me the same "original" idea that many said they'd gotten from their mothers or grandmothers. The similarities in "lazy" housecleaning techniques are amazing, and there's a good reason for that—they work!

In this book you'll find everything you need to know to keep a clean house without much effort, from lists of supplies and efficient ways to shop for them, to room by room cleaning "instruction," to advice on how to keep your house clean all the time. The first part of the book breaks down lists of cleaning supplies that you might consider purchasing and appliances that have more power than your mop and broom. Section two offers shopping tips and shortcuts to make cleaning up super simple. The main part of the book relays easy instructions for cleaning room by room. Each of these chapters starts with advice on how to sort the clutter before you start to put it away. You'll find that some of it will end up in the trash can, and the rest will be stored in a logical and convenient place. Oftentimes, underneath all the debris, you'll find a surprisingly clean room; it's the junk that makes it look like a mess.

On almost every page I offer a tried and true tip, from shortcuts to warnings. "Quick n' Painless" presents easy shortcuts for doing something even faster when you're really pressed for time. "You'll Thank Yourself Later" is exactly that: If you follow my advice, you'll save time and effort down the road. "A Complete Waste Of Time" offers three warnings against spending hours fixing what should never have been messed up in the first place. "If You're So Inclined" presents suggestions for times when you have a bit more energy and want to add a final touch to a completed task that might simply make something more attractive or comfortable.

"The Lazy Way" is your reward for a yeoman's effort and a job well done. Because you should never feel like you're working too hard!

Spiced with humor and easy step by step directions on how to put your home in apple pie order, *Clean Your House The Lazy Way* is meant to become your new best friend. So leave the guilt and stress behind, and start learning how to keep a clean house and enjoy life, too. There's no time like the present!

THANK YOU. . .

If it hadn't been for my darling husband, Peter, I probably would have thought more than twice about taking on this project. His constant encouragement, sidelines cheerleading, and invaluable proofreading, carried me through every phase of this manuscript.

Thank you to the rest of my family for their encouragement, and to friends and coworkers for sharing their helpful cleaning hints.

But most of all to Amy Gordon, my wonderful editor and creator of this new, exciting series: Thank you for admiring my homekeeping skills, for your faith in my abilities, and for your unlimited patience. You are a delight to work with and the best daughter a mother ever had.

Part 1

The Teeny Tidy Tool Box

Are You Too Lazy to Read the Teeny Tidy Tool Box?

1 Your broom handle still has a neat price sticker on it. ☐ yes ☐ no

2 You've taken "all-purpose cleaner" a bit too literally, considering that's the only bottle of cleaning solution you own. ☐ yes ☐ no

3 The last time you changed the vacuum cleaner bag was during the Carter administration. ☐ yes ☐ no

Mother Hubbard Meets Father Clean

Walking down the grocery store aisles and seeing the stock and variety of cleaning supplies just boggles my mind. This is too overwhelming for such an under-whelming task. So I use the KISS theory: Keep It Simple, Stupid.

I don't know about you, but I really don't have enough space in my kitchen cupboards for an extensive variety of cleaning products. By necessity, this kitchen space also needs to accommodate all the polishes and sprays that are needed for the living room, dining room, and family room. So I have to keep the number of products small but the quantity of each great (which I'll talk about later).

This is where shopping at one of those large, discount warehouses really pays off. (Unlike when you buy 10 pounds of potatoes that seem to grow eyes faster than you can blink your own.) I've become an aficionado of the discount warehouse; I shop only two to three times a year for my most frequently used cleaning supplies. The supplies come in bulk, vat, or "two-fer" sizes.

The up side of warehouse shopping is the infrequency with which you need to go. The downside is that bulk is bulky, and heavy, and awkward to handle. (I recommend that if you do buy bulk, save previously purchased "grocery-store sized" containers and refill them, but I'll talk more about that later.) Just make sure you have storage space, like in the basement or garage, for the large tubs and jugs.

If you don't have a shopping warehouse near you (which means you must live on a remote island), your local supermarket should suffice. If you're a coupon cutter by nature, cut coupons for tried-and-true products that you know get the job done, or for new products that you are curious to try.

As you read on, you'll see that my time-saver plan calls for expending the least amount of energy possible when zipping through your cleaning chores. I've discovered that if you can store the cleaning supplies within the room you are cleaning, you save time and unnecessary steps.

Unfortunately, the best game plans sometimes don't work out. So you punt. I do not have any place in my living room or dining room to keep cleaning paraphernalia. (Building a centerpiece around the can of Pledge didn't work.) So my dinky kitchen cupboard has to do for everything I need for the entire downstairs, excluding the powder room. My strategy: store fewer product types in greater quantity, and hone your refilling skills.

In Chapter 3, there are tips on how to buy in bulk, and organize and store your loot for the future. You'll discover that there are many more places than the kitchen cupboard and under the sink to conceal the cache.

To get you started, I've listed some of the cleaning supplies that you'll find handy to have stored in each room. In most cases, the products are for use in that particular room, but in some instances, they are things that you'll need in adjacent rooms as well—those that have no place within your decorating scheme for this purpose. (For brand names and descriptions of cleaning products, see "If You Don't Know What it Does, Look Here.")

IN THE KITCHEN

These are the items that I've found to be necessities for cleaning up the kitchen, living room, family room/den, and dining room. The list is not that long, not only because I have to store them in a kitchen cupboard (I envy those of you who have pantries, roomy or otherwise), but also because you really don't need that much.

Under the Sink

If you don't have enough room under your sink, keep the supplies in your garage, basement, or other secondary storage area. If you just don't have any extra space, choose only the items you consider most useful to put there. Also, take a hard look at what's taking up all that precious room, and get rid of non-essentials.

A COMPLETE WASTE OF TIME

The Three Worst Things to Do with Coupons:

1. Cut coupons for the sake of cutting coupons.

2. Take coupons to discount warehouses—unless you've checked to see if they accept them.

3. Save coupons to use at a later date—like most things in life, eventually they expire.

- Dishwasher detergent

- Dishwashing detergent

- Refill for hand soap dispenser

- Refill for the window cleaner

- Scouring pads with self-contained soap

- Scouring pads with no soap

- Sponges

- Extra garbage bags for the kitchen garbage can

- Big black garbage bags that you use on garbage day

- Rubber gloves

- Extra roll of paper towels

In the Cupboard

These are the big guns of housecleaning. With these few products you can mount a major assault on dirt, grime, spills, stains, and anything else that messes up your home. If you're short on cupboard space, banish any second-team products to another storage area, or get rid of them.

- Window cleaner in refillable spray bottle

- Floor cleaning product for your type of floor

- Bleaching cleanser

- Pine cleanser

- Mildew cleaner, if you have wall tile in your kitchen

- Paper towels (one roll in addition to the one on the towel rack)

- Spray stain cleaner for carpets

- Metal polish
- Old English Furniture Polish, a terrific liquid that hides scratches
- White vinegar (It's not just for salads anymore! Vinegar is a great deodorizer and a cleaning tool. Chapter 8 lists several uses for vinegar.)

In the Broom Closet

I do not have an actual broom closet in my kitchen. I have a closet in my family room that is the perfect size to store items that would go into a genuine "broom closet." You could also hang these items on hooks going down the basement staircase. These are things that just naturally seem to go together for convenient storage.

- Angle broom
- Dustpan
- Feather duster
- Vacuum cleaner, if there is room

IN THE LIVING ROOM

Moving right along. . . here are a few additional items that you'll need when you're cleaning the living room, especially if you have wood furniture. This room does not easily lend itself to storing cleaning products. So, you'll probably find yourself going into your kitchen and grabbing the window cleaner and paper towels and then picking up the vacuum and feather duster from where they're kept. Some sort of tote with handles would be a

QUICK 🖦 PAINLESS

If you're interested in another step saver, you can get a broom and dustpan unit—the dustpan handle fits snugly onto the broom stick. That way, the pan is always there when you need it!

great time saver, here. Throw everything you need into the carrier and take it to the rooms that are not set up for cleaning-ware storage.

- Murphy's Oil Soap
- Cleaner for wood furniture

IN THE BATHROOMS

Do you know anyone who smiles at the mention of cleaning the bathroom? I don't. The thought of purging this cubicle conjures images of Beetle Bailey on his hands and knees scrubbing the cold tile floor around the base of the latrine with nothing but a tooth brush.

You may have several bathrooms in your home. Some are easier to clean than others. The powder room is probably the easiest to keep in shape, since this room is usually used by guests or is a quick pit stop for family members. In most homes, this bathroom is smaller than the others and houses only a sink and a toilet. There's not too much to clean, but also not much space for storage.

For the Powder Room

If you've decorated your powder room with a pedestal sink—*très chic*. However, this does eliminate any under the sink storage. These rooms can sometimes be so tiny that storage space is really limited. In Chapter 3 you'll find some tips to rectify this situation, but, until then, here's a list of supplies to keep nearby.

- Floor cleaning product
- Bleaching cleanser

IF YOU'RE SO INCLINED

If you asked my husband, he would tell you that you need a toilet plunger in every bathroom. I say that you need the plumber's number next to every phone. Let's compromise and say that you should have at least one plunger that you can take where it's needed.

- Toilet bowl cleanser
- Toilet brush
- Window or mirror spray
- Paper towels (one roll)
- One sponge
- Several rolls of toilet paper (or "tissue" to be politically correct)

For the Master Bath

The list of cleaning products you'll need for this bathroom is quite a bit longer than the one designed for the powder room. But we're not just talking sink and a toilet, here. In most cases, your master bath will be a much larger room. The features can range from a simple bathtub to a jacuzzi, from a stall shower to a steam, from a regular toilet to a separate area for toilet and bidet. The number of products grows in direct proportion to the number of bathroom fixtures that you have. Chapter 9 will walk you through the steps of creating a simple cleaning routine.

- Floor cleaning product
- Bleaching cleanser
- Toilet bowl cleanser
- Mildew cleaner
- Soap scum cleaner
- Drain cleaner
- Toilet brush
- Window or mirror spray

QUICK ⟨ɴ⟩ PAINLESS

Instead of scrubbing those nasty stains on the inside of the toilet bowl, try one of the varieties of cleaners that sit inside of the tank and work each time you flush. Some are tablets that you drop into the tank and others hang inside the tank from a hook that you attach to the edge. Sounds good to me! (Keep the lid down so that animals and kids won't get into the chemicals.)

- Roll of paper towels
- Two sponges
- Cotton swabs
- Several rolls of toilet tissue
- Extra box of facial tissue
- Several boxes of hand and bath-size soap

For the Kids' Bathroom

This room is going to be your greatest challenge, especially if you are toilet training. Little people can have big accidents. And little hands have troubles with buttons, zippers, and snaps. Just remember, not everyone is a straight shooter. Also be sure that you place all cleaning products far out of reach of curious eyes and little hands. If this bathroom has a linen closet, consider using the top shelf for this type of storage. There are also kid-proof locks that can be attached to cupboard doors. If in doubt, remove anything that might cause harm to another room.

- Floor cleaning product
- Bleaching cleanser
- Toilet bowl cleanser
- Mildew cleaner
- Soap scum cleaner
- Drain cleaner
- Toilet brush
- Window or mirror spray

- Roll of paper towels
- Two sponges
- Cotton swabs for those little hard-to-reach places
- Toothpicks
- Two extra hand and bath soaps
- Two rolls of toilet paper
- Two boxes of tissues
- Toilet plunger

IN THE BASEMENT

Whether your basement is finished with carpeting and paneling or is old and dingy and somewhat spooky, all that you need are a few hardy shelves that can handle the large refill bottles and products that you haven't been able to fit in any other room. This is also the area for seldom-used supplies. If you find that you're running down to the basement, regularly, for a specific item, find a place for it that is closer at hand.

- Chlorine bleach
- Paper towels
- Sponges
- Wide push broom
- Regular size broom
- Dustpan
- Mop
- Pail
- Rags

QUICK n' PAINLESS

Check out the hardware stores, the housewares section of the grocery store, or even infomercials on television for the dusters that have an extension arm that grabs dust and cobwebs from those hard-to-reach areas.

IN THE GARAGE

Shelving and pegboards are a boon to garage organization. They prevent all of you garage "stuff" from being lost, disorganized, or run over by your sixteen year old son who just got his driver's permit.

- Wide push broom
- Dust pan
- Hose
- Spray nozzle

Now you know what cleaning products to buy in bulk for each room, and where to store them. In Chapter 3 you get to know the ins and outs of shopping in bulk, getting your stock home, and putting it away in useable quantities.

Getting Time on Your Side

	The Old Way	The Lazy Way
Organizing coupons	30 minutes	3 minutes
Storing cleaning supplies	15 minutes	5 minutes
Wasting time looking for cleaning item	10 minutes	0 minutes
Waiting on the throne while someone runs to get another roll of toilet paper	5 minutes	0 minutes (there are 4 extra rolls under the sink!)
Driving back to the store to get the window cleaner you forgot	30 minutes	0 minutes (you have 3 bottles!)
Scrubbing the stain off the counter with regular soap and water	10 minutes	0 minutes (you have the right cleaner!)

Chapter two

Power Provisions

Whether you're buying a winter coat or a vacuum cleaner, you're going to look for a salesperson who gives you his undivided attention.

When I buy clothing, for example, I have a tendency to shop in small specialty boutiques rather than in large department stores. I'm usually in a hurry, and I find it so much easier to walk into a shop where I know the salespeople and they know me. They understand what kind of clothing I like, and what looks good on me; I don't have to waste time explaining myself and trying on items that I would never be caught dead in. I apply this same philosophy to appliances, including vacuum cleaners.

I explain to the salesperson that I know what features I want; I don't know the technical terms and I certainly couldn't care less about what's going on under the hood.

The last vacuum I purchased was almost two years ago when my old cleaner suddenly died two days before my daughter's wedding and the day before her fiancé's parents were coming for dinner. I literally ran into the Vacuum

Cleaner Center bellowing, "Help me," and Bob, the owner, started to explain features to me. I stopped him mid sentence and said, "just sell me what you think is the best cleaner for me, knowing my lifestyle and family." It was probably the fastest sale he ever made. I signed the credit card slip while Bob loaded my brand new teal-colored Sanyo into the trunk of my car. That weekend produced two marriages made in heaven: my daughter and son-in-law and me and my new vacuum cleaner.

Letting the clerk do the work is only one way to shop for cleaning equipment that's right for you. If you know something about vacuum cleaners and like to do your own research, you can read up on what's available in appliance store catalogs, check out ratings in *Consumer Reports,* see what's on your home shopping networks, or visit some Internet shopping sites. Or you just might like to browse and look at what's available in the flesh (or metal, to be exact). Asking friends about how happy they are with their new Orecks isn't a bad idea either.

VA-VA-VA-VOOM VACUUMS

My visit to the Village Vacuum Cleaner Center gave me the opportunity to meet Lynn, the Bag Lady. Believe me, this lady ain't no bag: quite a looker, very nice and extremely helpful. She gave me the real Cook's Tour into the land of power provisions and the various carpet and floor cleaning tools. (And, no, Lynn is not homeless. She keeps track of which bags fit which vacuum cleaners and will even deliver them to your door. All she needs is a phone call.)

Uprights Are No Slouches

This vacuum looks like the one that Beaver Cleaver's mother used as she swept through the house in her four-inch high heels, shirt-dress enhanced with several starched crinolines, and the prettily and perfectly ironed apron covering the whole ensemble. June did not lean over, drag, or sweat. She gracefully waltzed around the room, picking up what little dust the perfect American family created. However, Mrs. Cleaver's vacuum was no match for the remarkable variety of cleaners on the market today.

The upright style is shaped like an "L" with the beaters encased in a housing on the floor; the handle stands up at a 90-degree angle from the beater housing. The handle extends to about waist high and the bag fits into an enclosed section in front of the handle.

My style of upright stores the attachments right in the back of the vacuum itself. They call it "tools on board." There are even little diagrams etched into the back of the vacuum that show you the compartment where these tools fit for storage. In this model, the hose is permanently attached to the machine and snaps into its own space when not in use. The wand, or extender rod, disassembles into two pieces that also snap into their marked compartments in the casing. Basic attachment tools are:

- **The crevice tool:** flat and angled. Like all of the attachments, it fits onto the end of the wand. The crevice tool is able to squeeze into the corners of your sofa and chairs and eat up the cracker crumbs and dog hairs that are hidden there. It also sneaks

YOU'LL THANK YOURSELF LATER

You take your car in several times a year for a lube job, don't you? Then why not your vacuum cleaner? This motor needs an oil change just as much as your auto does. A check-up, once a year, will save you a lot of grief and money in the long run. A good maintenance plan will prevent a burned out motor or catch a vacuum cleaner belt before it's ready to snap. It also might save you a frantic trip to Bob's store.

into the curves of your moldings to grab anything that lives there and sucks it away.

- **The dusting brush:** either round or oval shaped with bristles around the circumference and a hole in the center from which the suction is drawn.

- **The upholstery tool:** features a nozzle three to four inches wide and a lip that is cantilevered about one inch. As the name proclaims, its responsibility is to glide across your fabric-covered furniture slurping up dust, pet hairs, and the like.

Lynn, the "Bag Lady," recommended that when buying a new vacuum cleaner you should consider a model that has a self-adjusting head. This feature allows you to run directly from carpet to floor and vice versa without physically having to adjust the machine. A lot of manufacturers are moving toward these self-adjusting appliances.

Cuddly, Carefree Canisters

Want a pet but the landlord won't allow it? Or perhaps your spouse is allergic? Then buy a canister vacuum cleaner. It sits close to the ground and looks like a small, round animal with a long tail. (The tail is the slinky-like, flexible hose to which the three basic attachments are affixed.) It may not snuggle with you on the sofa or play fetch in the backyard, but at least you don't have to clean up after it—it actually cleans up after you!

A good number of canister vacuums are made solely to do bare floors and details, such as upholstery, crevices,

and general dusting. These aforementioned canisters are lightweight and are marketed for vacuuming stairs, as well as cleaning your car interior. If you buy one of these models, however, be prepared to purchase an additional machine for carpets.

When choosing a canister appliance, be sure to check out both the air-driven as well as the motor-driven models:

IF YOU'RE SO
INCLINED

- An air-driven system is preferable because it's easy to add attachments.
- A motor-driven system requires you to disconnect parts before adding the attachments.

If you like the canister approach to vacuuming but cannot afford two machines, have no space to store two machines, or just don't like the concept of two machines, look into the canister with a turbo brush to clean the rugs. This apparatus is lightweight, easy to use on the stairs, and is ideal for you if heavy lifting is not in your program.

Grand Central Convenience Vac

Believe it or not, many new homes are built with a central vacuum cleaner system. Every room has a round opening in the baseboard into which the hose is connected. This opening leads to a shaft that conducts the debris down to the bowels of the basement and into the great suction pot, the heart and soul of the mechanism. (This sounds a little like liposuction, doesn't it?) The 30-foot vacuum cleaner hose that serves as an extension of

There are some canister vacuums on the market that do not require vacuum cleaner bags. You simply open them up and dump out the dirt. If dollar savings are what you're after, this is your baby. If maintenance and time are what you are looking for, I suggest that you stick to the bag type equipment. Bagless canisters get messy when you dump them, and you're going to end up cleaning up the clean up.

Vacuum Central is portable. As you go from room to room, you unhook the hose and reattach it in the succeeding chamber. In addition to the conduit, the attachments also have to be transferred from room to room. (Don't worry—in Chapter 5, "Keep It Clean Without Becoming the Maid," I discuss what to do when faced with transporting utilities from room to room.)

There is a neat attachment that you may wish to consider for a Central Vac System. It's called a Rug Rat; a small rotary brush that is used for cleaning upholstery and stairs.

The Great Brush Roller Debate

This is a subject that takes some serious consideration when you're buying a vacuum cleaner. Did you ever think you'd be pondering this topic? Me either. But here it goes. There are three types of brush rollers:

- **Plastic:** The plastic brush rollers have a plastic-on-plastic construction and have a tendency to melt or warp within one to three years.

Brush Roller	Price range of vacuum cleaner	Estimated Life of brush roller	Approximate cost of replacement
Plastic	Basic economy under $200	Average of 1 to 3 years	Could run up to $120
Metal	Over $200	Average of 5 years	@ $25
Wood	Over $200	Average of 5 years	@ $25

- **Metal:** These brush rollers have a longer life than the plastic.
- **Wood:** The wood brush rollers have a longer life than the plastic.

This chart may help give you a little insight as to why various vacuums differ in price according to the material used to construct the brush roller. Different rollers have a different life span as well as a wide range in replacement costs. Ask your salesperson to go over these details in the models that he/she recommends.

Buying a vacuum cleaner sounds a little like buying a car, huh? Next thing you'll be wondering is how long will it be until you turn it in for a new model.

POWER PUFF PROVISION PACIFIERS

When all you need is a "quicker picker upper," a lighter weight electric broom or hand vac will solve your cleaning needs. These models are colorful, streamlined, and easy to use.

Easygoing Electric Brooms

Some of the smaller power provisions are adorable. Okay, adorable may not be the right word for a piece of cleaning equipment to you. But considering that the electric broom I use was purchased in 1964, these new lightweight, colorful, attractive, battery-powered or electric-cord-powered cleaning tools are wonderful, and, yes, adorable. When you shop for an electric broom, consider the features of each type.

QUICK PAINLESS

To eliminate the battle-of-the-fringe on your area rug, and to prevent your sheer window treatments from being sucked up into the vacuum cleaner bag, buy a vacuum with a suction regulator on the hose. This feature is found on several models.

The features of a **rechargeable battery-powered electric broom:**

- Easily portable
- Lightweight (about five pounds)
- Cleans carpets, as well as bare floors
- Safe for children to use
- Easy for seniors or youngsters to use

The features of an **electric broom with an electric-cordpower source:**

- Lightweight (about five pounds)
- Cleans carpets, as well as bare floors.
- Must be plugged in each room in which you use it
- Not for use by young children
- Easy for seniors to use

Both types of electric brooms will do a terrific job. The only difference is the battery source. If you have young children and want them to be able to use the machine, or if you are a senior who has difficulty bending over, then the battery powered broom will probably be preferable to your life style. Remember, though, it's just like your cell phone—it only works when the battery is charged. You have to have a place to store the broom that has an electrical source available for charging.

I don't know if every store would let you take the power provision home for a day or two to test it on your own carpets and floors, but it never hurts to ask. You might also want to question what happens if you really hate your purchase after you've used it two or three times. Is there a guarantee? Is there an exchange or return policy, or is it like when you buy a car—the minute you sign the papers and drive it out of the lot, the lemon is yours? If you can't test it out at home, ask to test out the appliance in the store.

Hassle-free Hand Vacs

As with electric brooms, these, too, come in the cord and cordless variety. Again, the cordless vacs are rechargeable. A few chores that you can readily accomplish with a hand vac are:

- Vacuum the stairs
- Vacuum your car's interior
- Vacuum your car's trunk
- Pick up spilled, non-liquid items
- Pick up the hair on your bathroom floor

A hand vac does the same chores as the electric broom, but it's a little awkward to use. While you stand upright when sweeping with the broom, you have to bend over when you use the hand vac. Since it is a little awkward, if you intend for your child to use this, I recommend that you see first if he can handle this appliance.

A Blast from the Past

Let's see if you can guess what this is: It's neither a plug-in nor rechargeable. It's:

- Lightweight
- Small and compact
- Safe for kids
- Handy for seniors
- Picks up dirt, doesn't sweep it

QUICK ⬛ PAINLESS

Black and Decker makes something called the Spillbuster, a cordless, handheld vacuum that's made to slurp up liquid spills. No more crying over spilt milk.

It's a carpet sweeper! Believe it or not, they are still available. They are not expensive, are easy to store, and best of all, they work.

Totally and Decadently Easygoing—The Mop Vac

Tired of taking out the mop and the bucket when it's time to wash your kitchen floor? Then look into a mop-vac. There's no mop, no bucket, no bending, no dunking, no wringing, no twisting. It's electric. The mop vac exhales the cleaning solutions and then inhales the dirt while simultaneously sucking up the liquid.

The mop vac is a relatively new product on the market. A small downside is that you have to use the manufacturer's cleaning solution. In other words, your regular floor cleaner is not the product of choice for this power appliance. Check it out at your local appliance store.

BAGS AND THE BAG LADY

At the start of this chapter, I mentioned Lynn, my Bag Lady at the Village Vacuum Cleaner Center. The Bag Lady is a terrific customer service offered by the store. Ask if your store has this service.

Just as there are different models, styles, and manufacturers of vacuum cleaners, there are different models, styles, and manufacturers of vacuum cleaner bags. When you buy the vacuum, the store usually gives you a few extra bags. But, one day, inevitably, the supply runs out. So, you jot down "vacuum cleaner bags" on your shopping list. The next time you're in the grocery store, you go to grab the bags. And there you stand, pensively. You discover that in order to buy the right bag, you have to know the right brand, model, and style of your vacuum. Model? You can't even recall the make.

So you probably do one of three things: 1. Go home, pull out your vacuum, copy down the information, and go back to the supermarket, 2. Decide to forget it for now and wait until the next time you shop (which means if you need to use the vacuum between now and then, the only purpose it will serve is building up your arm muscle), or 3. Take a wild guess and grab what you think looks like it will fit your model, which of course is the wrong choice. What a waste of time!

Not with the Bag Lady! When I run out of bags, I call the Bag Lady at the Vacuum Cleaner Center. And guess what? They deliver the bags I need directly to my doorstep!

MAKE A CLEANER SWEEP

Here are a few additional tips that will set you on a course of hassle-free housecleaning.

IF YOU'RE SO
INCLINED

Ask the vacuum or general appliance store you deal with if they provide a Bag Lady service. If they don't, suggest that they do!

- Take your vacuum cleaner and other power tools in for a check up once a year. Maintenance only takes about three days and can save you a lot of time, money, and aggravation in the long run.

- Be sure that yearly maintenance includes having your machine's bearings greased.

- Have the vacuum cleaner belt changed about every six months. The belt costs about $1.99, not that much compared to the price of replacing a burned-out motor.

Buy your power provisions from a store

1. that listens to your needs,

2. whose salespeople are knowledgeable,

3. whose salespeople are willing to take the time to explain the products to you,

4. where they don't push a specific brand or model, and

5. that has great customer service.

HOOVER'S LITTLE HELPERS

While you are shopping for vacuums and bags, look at these handy dandy products. They were highly recommended and work in conjunction with your vacuum to make your cleaning free and easier.

- Stain-X Carpet Stain Remover

- Gonzo Pet Hair Lifter

- Allergy Micro Bags: They pick up infinitesimal specks of dust in an effort to alleviate allergy symptoms. (The standard bags that are made for my vacuum cleaner are of this type.)

Getting Time On Your Side

	The Old Way	The Lazy Way
Vacuuming the stairs	10 minutes	4 minutes
Unplugging the carpet fringe	3 minutes	0 minutes
Looking for vacuum cleaner attachment	6 minutes	0 minutes
Mopping up spills	3 minutes	1 minute
Picking up bathroom hair	3 minutes	1 Minute
Driving to the store to return the wrong size vacuum bags	40 minutes	0 minutes (hoorah for the bag lady!)

Part 2

Spiffy in a Jiffy

Are You Too Lazy to Read Spiffy in a Jiffy?

1 Your recurring dream is about winning a "Maid for a Day."
☐ yes ☐ no

2 Your youngest son said watching Dad try to clean up was better than watching MTV. ☐ yes ☐ no

3 You've called around to try to find a self-cleaning microwave.
☐ yes ☐ no

three

Shop, Stock, Store, and Siesta

Our family is quite large and seems to be expanding every day. All 10 adults hold down pressure-cooker jobs. In addition, one is in grad school, one is a medical resident, two have infants, one is expecting, one travels weekly, two have three dogs, one has one cat, one is allergic to all animals, three are fixing up newly purchased homes, one is a Martha-Stewart-do-alike, two are single and working at a social life, one plays golf with a passion, two own their own businesses, and the two most mature people of this gaggle of grown-ups are parents, grandparents, and in-laws of all of the above.

What does this have to do with housecleaning, you ask? Unfortunately, housecleaning is a part of life and each of us handles life in his or her own way. Some of us are Type-A personalities, others are Type-B. Some of us work well under pressure, and others would crumble under pressure on a regular basis. Though we live very different lives, we are all juggling tasks, and we all want to find easier, faster ways to get routine things done. So much to do, so little time, and house-cleaning is no exception.

Along the way I've learned some things about how to save time when housecleaning, and still do a great job. These are some tips I've given my children on how to shop for and store cleaning products so they can save many unnecessary steps, and spend more time doing other things.

But before you jump into your car and zoom to the supermarket, take a minute to look around and decide what you're going to do with the loot once you have it home. You're going to be shopping big. Leaving the bags on the kitchen floor until you work your way through the supplies is not a good storage plan. So before you do anything else, take this opportunity to get rid of unnecessary, old, and useless items that have been cluttering up your shelves for months. Start with a clean sweep; no pun intended .

SHOP SMART

Shopping smart means making fewer trips to the supermarket. It also means you can spend more time doing the things that you enjoy doing.

Buy in Quantity

Open up your mind. Think big! If you have a general idea of what you would use in a week, multiply that by twelve and you've got a three-month supply.

Paper the House

As you may have read in Chapter 1, "Mother Hubbard

A COMPLETE WASTE OF TIME

The Three Worst Things to Do When Buying in Bulk:

1. Buy products you've never tried.

2. Automatically buy the cheapest brand—bulk means bargain!

3. Buy on impulse. You don't like it? Well, you're stuck with a five-pound jug.

Meets Mr. Clean," I suggest that you buy cleaning products in bulk. A membership to one of the many discount warehouses will really pay off, not only in dollars, but in time.

If you don't shop at a discount store, watch for sales at your local grocery store and then stock up. What a good feeling it is to know that if both the women's Olympic swim and basketball teams come to call, you are sufficiently stocked with toilet paper. (I haven't had the pleasure of housing these teams, but when all the members of our family descend as weekend guests, it certainly seems like it.)

- Buy toilet paper (toilet tissue if you want to be genteel) by the case. Also buy tissues in as many boxes as the manufacturer can bundle together. I see no point in box-by-box or roll-by-roll purchasing. You can substitute toilet paper for tissues and vice versa, but what happens when you run out of both?!

- Buy paper towels in eight-, 12-, and 15-roll bulk packs. Don't waste time on the two-packs. Although the two-packs may seem like a bargain, you actually end up spending more money on them than on the larger quantity packs. And they run out faster so you're always making hurried trips to the store.

Spray It Away

I always try to buy certain cleaning liquids in bulk. When I talk about "bulk" in this instance, I mean vast vats, colossal containers that are awkward and heavy as heck. Now, if you played football in high school, you probably won't have a problem lifting, opening, pouring, and closing these jugs (and would perhaps consider it your workout for the week). But I, on the other hand, though slightly larger in stature than Dr. Ruth, have difficulty moving these containers from the grocery shelf to my shopping cart. There is no way that I want to hoist them on a regular basis. Some things to keep in mind:

- Some products do not come in super large sizes, but you can purchase decent sized refill bottles.

- Hold on to the spray bottles and refill them as they become empty. Why keep buying spray bottles of window cleaner every time you run out? You're paying for the spray attachment.

Shop Once; Buy Twice

If you read the shopping list for cleaning products in Chapter 1, I'm sure you noticed that I recommend that you put the same types of cleaners in several different rooms. For example, window cleaner: a spray bottle in the kitchen cupboard, a refill bottle under the sink, and additional spray bottles in each bathroom. I probably have at least one or two more refills stored in the basement.

Write It Down

Before you go shopping, make a list of exactly what you will need. This may take a few extra minutes, but you won't get home to discover that you forgot something and have to go back to the store.

The easiest way to prevent backtracking may be to devise a chart outlining the various kinds of cleaning

Don't throw out the small plastic containers and spray bottles that you've been using for pine cleaner, dishwashing detergent, etc. Refill them, as you need to from the mammoth drums in your storage area.

supplies you'll be using in each room of your home. (You may want to refer to Chapter 1 of this book as a guide.) The chart below is a watered down version of what you'll probably be buying, but it should give you the idea.

Now simply check off in the vertical columns what you plan on using for each room. Then total them horizontally, putting the numbers in the "Total" column. These totals represent the number of each item you need to buy for your immediate use.

Cleaning Supplies

	Kitchen	Powder Room	Master Bath	Total
Window spray cleaner	x	x	x	3
Dishwasher detergent	x			1
Dishwashing detergent	x			1
Sponges	x	x	x	3
Bleaching cleanser	x	x	x	3
Pine cleanser	x			1
Mildew cleaner			x	1
Paper towels	x	x	x	3
Murphy's Oil Soap	x			1

If you find the chart useful, create one on your computer, print it out, and place it on the fridge. Or just make one by hand.

Fill the Cart

Buy enough bottles (or extra spray bottles) to place in the cupboards of every room in your house. Stock the kitchen, each bathroom, and some closets with all the cleaning supplies that you will need in that particular room. Everything will be at your fingertips—no running up and down the stairs carrying armfuls of supplies. A real time and energy saver!

Buy more than you need for immediate consumption. For example, when you get to the window cleaner section, pick up three spray bottles and two to three large refills. Throw the same number of bleaching cleansers and sponges into your cart. If the chart total calls for one, you really should grab two to three. When you toss in one of the 15-packs of paper towels, you're all set. There, you've started the process of buying in bulk.

The next time you need these items, months down the road, your shopping cart will look leaner. Since you already own the spray bottles, all you'll need to pick up are refills. Voilá!

My husband is a quantity shopping pro. He fills one cart, leaves it at the check-out counter, picks up a second cart, and continues on his spree. He's never been to a discount warehouse. Given that his vehicle of choice is a truck, I shudder at the thought of the damage he could do if he used the flatbed carts that these stores provide. (Warning to all you novice quantity shoppers: if you're a two-cart shopper, like my husband is, always let the clerk at the check out know what you're doing. Otherwise, you might find all the items that filled your first cart back on the shelves!)

Load it Up

As I see it, the two advantages of discount warehouse shopping are the dollar savings and the institutional and commercial sizes available for purchase. The downside is that warehouse shopping is no-frills shopping. In some stores, there are no conveyor belts on which to place your purchases. The checker takes an item out of your cart, scans it, and places it into another cart—the one that you take to your car. There are no baggers; in fact, there are no bags. Boxes may be available near the check out or throughout the store, but it is first come, first served. And don't bother looking for someone to help you to load your car.

Bulk shopping can be fun. It just pays to be prepared and know what to expect. Here are a few pointers that will make you look and feel like a pro your first time out:

- Throw a few cardboard boxes and paper or plastic bags in the car before you leave for the warehouse store.
- Unload the items from your shopping cart directly into the receptacles. Grocery items won't roll around the trunk and you'll save steps when you unload your car.

YOU'LL THANK YOURSELF LATER

To speed up putting away your groceries, organize them as you load up your car. Place all of the items that get stored in the basement into one box, those that go into the kitchen cupboard into another carton, the powder room items into another, and so on. Then, simply unload the car and walk your cargo directly to its storage place.

To make shopping even easier, choose a grocery store that has a "grocery valet." After you've paid for your purchase, go to the parking lot for your car, drive to the grocery pick up area, pop your trunk, and let the valet pack your car. Never thought you could feel pampered at the supermarket, huh?

THE WAREHOUSE ALTERNATIVE: EXPLORE THE SUPERSTORE

If, in your mind, convenience outweighs price, after a warehouse, the supermarket is the next best place to pick up cleaning supplies. The supermarket superstores carry a wide selection of products at a variety of price points. You won't find the institutional sizes, but you can take the philosophy of "shop once, buy twice" to a higher level. Since quantities will be smaller, you may want to consider buying more units of an item to store away for later use.

Some of the larger supermarkets in different parts of the country, A&P for example, do stock many of the supersized items, especially in the paper products department. In fact, they're often featured at great prices—better than the warehouse stores. Maybe this is a growing trend?

Convenient Conveyors

When you put your groceries onto the check-out conveyor, organize them by room. Arrange all the items that get stored in the basement together, those that go into the kitchen cupboard together, the powder room, and so on. You can indicate to the checker who bags them as they come off the conveyor that you've grouped your items and would like them to be bagged that way. Most clerks are happy to comply. This is really helpful when you unload your car at home. You'll be able to simply carry your bags directly to where their contents will be stored.

Put It Away

Never take two steps when one step will do. If you already semi-organized your groceries at the store or in your trunk, you're halfway home. Carry the bags to their storage place, unload, and then don't think about shopping for cleaning supplies for several months. If this is your maiden voyage as a bulk shopper, there are a few effortless steps I'll walk you through.

1. If you haven't saved any empty plastic spray bottles, skip to 5. If you have, line them up on the kitchen table.

2. Check the shopping list you used, and determine how many bottles you need for window cleaner, bleaching cleanser, and so on.

3. Group the spray bottles together as to kind.

4. Fill each bottle from the large refill container.

5. Sort the various items according to the rooms in which they belong.

6. Add the right number of sponges, rolls of paper towels, toilet paper, and boxes of tissue to the piles.

7. Place each pile of items into a grocery bag or another receptacle and, making just one trip to each storage location, put the items away.

From Store to Storage

You've made your shopping list, gone to the store, loaded and unloaded the car, organized your purchases and carried the items, in a very few number of trips, to

YOU'LL THANK YOURSELF LATER

If you're refilling plastic spray bottles, use a bottle with the right label, or be sure to remove the wrong label and re-label it with the name of the bottle's actual contents to avoid mix-ups. You wouldn't want to use Murphy Oil Soap on your windows.

their storage sites. Have you put the cart before the horse? Storage space doesn't just happen; you have to create it. Here are a few ideas to get you started:

- Clean out the cupboards in which you plan to store the goods. Check your designated kitchen cupboard, under the sink, and in the vanities under the bathroom sinks for any unnecessary stuff that can be eliminated, e.g., the plant food that hardened in the plastic container, electric hair rollers that you haven't used since 1984, and half-filled bottles of cleaning supplies that never did the job.

- If you don't have ample storage space in the basement, you may want to think about installing shelves. If your hobby happens to be carpentry, you can build some beautiful wooden shelving along the wall. Otherwise, I recommend buying plastic stackable shelves. (The metal ones you have to put together yourself are a pain and always seem to tilt anyway.) You can even use milk crates if you like.

- You may want to visit a store that sells a variety of bins that can organize and harbor the cleaning products to get exactly what you need. Buy some small bins that fit under your sink so that you don't mix the scouring powder up with your exfoliant.

- Throw out anything you haven't used in the past year and that takes up space in the areas you have now designated for house cleaning products.

YOU'LL THANK YOURSELF LATER

If your groceries are in the trunk of your car, back the car into your garage and park it as close to your door as possible. You'll be surprised how many steps you'll save by not having to walk around to the back of the car each time you remove an armload of grocery bags.

The kitchen, each bathroom, and any closets should now have all the cleaning products that you need to get the job done. You have made great strides. Congratulations!

Getting Time on Your Side

	The Old Way	The Lazy Way
Trips to the grocery store for cleaning supplies	12 trips	1 trip
Running out of toilet paper	5 times	0–1 time
Running up and down the stairs to get supplies	3 times	0 times
Trips from the car to the house unloading groceries	20 trips	4 trips
Time wasted scrubbing because you ran out of the product that works	1 hour	0 minutes
Unloading the groceries	30 minutes	5–8 minutes

Sweep It Under the Rug: Shortcuts and Do-Ahead Tips

I **present you with a scenario:**

Three family members are relaxing, watching a video, and noshing. One is devouring popcorn with extra butter and sipping a soda. The second is force-feeding himself a three-inch thick hero dripping with extra mayo and washing it down with a glass of tomato juice with lemon. The last, the low-fat maven, is snacking on cherries and drinking bottled water. The movie ends, they rewind, and head off to beddy-bye.

When the sun raises it's smiling head, the rubble from last night's feasting is encrusted, caked, stiffened, hardened, and thickened on the coffee table. There are stains and crumbs and debris. What would have taken a few minutes of pick-up, rinse, and wipe is now a full-blown cleaning operation.

Yuck! Not for me.

PAINLESS PICK-IT-UPS

Do you like to cook? Do you have a recipe for which you are famous? When you finish preparing your creation does your kitchen look as though there's been a major food fight? Next time haute cuisine calls, try cleaning up, little by little, as you go. You'll thank yourself later!

Clean as You Go

My daughter and I love cooking together. We enjoy designing the menu, setting the table, experimenting with new recipes, working and laughing side-by-side. It's a real mother-daughter moment. And what makes it truly succeed is that my daughter can always count on me to clean up the drips and spills as we go. If she puts down a spoon, I rinse it off and pop it into the dishwasher. If something boils over, I'm right there with my trusty sponge to make the glop disappear. Paper towel in one hand, wooden spoon in the other, in the kitchen, I'm a dirt devil.

I know that most of us don't cook in tandem. And little dirt devils don't follow us around the kitchen. But we can make the clean-up process move quicker and end sooner by taking little steps like popping utensils into the dishwasher when we finish using them, instead of piling them all in the sink, only to deal with a loud, tangled mess of pots and pans afterward.

Cleaning as you go isn't just for the kitchen—it is a terrific method of saving steps and eliminating piles of stuff from collecting in every room of the house. Start with some of these tips and see if you don't notice a difference.

- Put dirty dishes directly into the dishwasher. No pit stops in the sink.

- Scrape and peel vegetables and fruits over the garbage can. Scraping them into the sink is an added step, and, in the case of many vegetable peels, not recommended for disposals, if you even have one.

- Toss your dirty clothes into the laundry hamper instead of a pile on the floor.

- Hang up your coat in the closet when you take it off instead of throwing it onto the chair.

- Sort your mail near a wastebasket. Toss the junk mail directly into the "circular file," the unsolicited catalogs into the recycling bin, and the bills into the payables drawer (or basket, or box), instead of leaving piles on the counter.

- Make the bed when you get out of it.

Create a Routine

I'm sure that there are many approaches to keeping house. One is to divide tasks into those you do daily, weekly, monthly, quarterly, and so on. My view of housecleaning is a little different. I don't really schedule anything. I routine it. Here are a few starter tips.

- Wipe it up before it hardens.

- Soak it out before it soils.

YOU'LL THANK YOURSELF LATER

Don't put off until tomorrow what you can do now. A quick pick-up, rinse, and put-it-away will save you scraping, scrubbing, and restoring in the morning. Believe me—you will thank yourself later.

- Pick it up before it collects dust.

- Cast it out before it's clutter.

- Put it away so it won't stray.

- Do it now save time later.

- Read on, McDuff, for timely tenets.

Address the Mess

Have you ever misplaced your glasses? The remote control? Your car keys? Your car? (Well, then you may have a bit more than cleanliness to worry about.) Why do articles always seem to be missing when you're in a hurry? Why is it getting harder to find anything that you're looking for lately? Is it under this pile, or that one?

Close your eyes and picture each of your rooms without the clutter, without the accumulations on the countertop, the dresser, and the end table. Think what it would be like being able to take a direct route from the bedroom to the bathroom without having to circumvent last week's laundry. Hosanna! You can do it! Take it one step at a time. Try one room at a time. Divide the procedure into two basic steps:

1. Attack the piles.

For instance:

- Pick up the clothes on the floor.

- Sort the mail.

- Throw out, or read and then throw out, last week's newspapers.

- Clean off the top of your dresser.

2. Make homes for wandering objects:

- **Your car keys.** I have a little basket sitting on a shelf in my kitchen. That's where I keep my car keys. (You may prefer a decorative hook next to the garage door or in the kitchen.) Whenever I come in from the garage, I put my keys into the basket. When it's time for a ride, I always know where to find them.

- **Your eyeglasses.** You can wear them on a chain around your neck, put them back into the case each time you take them off, or buy one of the table top holders: Some are Lucite and others are made of wood; they are vertical cube-like objects into which you place your glasses.

- **Shoes and boots.** Place a basket or other container near the front door. Shoes get tossed into the bin, the entranceway looks neat, and your floors and rugs stay clean.

- **The contents of your pant's pockets.** Gentlemen, try emptying your pants pockets into a basket that sits on top of your nightstand or on top of your dresser. You'll always know where your wallet or money clip is and you're ready to refill your pockets in the morning.

- **Purse.** If you get into the habit of placing your purse in your bedroom, or on a hook in the hall or closet, each time you come home, you'll never lose it and it won't become part of the kitchen clutter.

- **Cell phone.** Plug your cell phone into the charger that sits on top of your desk or the kitchen counter.

YOU'LL THANK YOURSELF LATER

Since we tend to use our eyeglasses in several different rooms, you may want to put a holder on your night-stand, in the den, and another in the kitchen. It certainly will limit your search.

Phones that lend themselves to doing double-duty are the cordless model or those with a long cord (at least 25 feet) and a shoulder cradle. If you have a speakerphone, you can really move around the room. The telephone that is the most conducive to double duty is the kind that looks like a head-set for a Walkman with a small mouth-piece attached. Depending on which generation you are a member of, you'll remind yourself of either a night club DJ or Ernestine, the Lily Tomlin character from "Laugh In"—"One ringy-dingy. Two ringy-dingy."

If you establish a pattern of "putting it away," whatever it is, and whenever you need it, you'll create harmony in your household. You'll be surprised how neat your surroundings have become, and with very little effort. Once you get the hang of it, I'll bet you won't even realize that you're straightening up. You'll simplify your life. Believe me, returning "it" to its proper place will save time and effort in the long run.

Do Double Duty Without Drudgery

Doing double duty is doing two things at the same time—multi-tasking, as I like to call it. I'll bet that if you think about it, you may already perform this feat. If you do, then you simply must learn to re-apply your dexterity and incorporate some cleaning chores into your double duty routine.

I do a great deal of double duty while talking on the telephone, mostly in the kitchen. I can load or empty the dishwasher, scrub a pot, clean out a silverware drawer, or set the table—or all of the above—while chatting on the phone. It just depends upon how many people I care to speak with. The monotony that you usually associate with housework seems to disappear, or at least dissipate. When you're doing something that you're glad to be getting done, your hands seem to work by rote, and before you know it, you've dealt with the chores you've been avoiding, and the guilt that went with it.

Try performing double duty while watching TV. For instance, you may find it more agreeable to fold and sort your laundry while you watch a movie than when you remove it from the dryer. Try these ideas on for size.

While watching TV:

- Write your cleaning supplies list.

- Clean out that drawer you keep complaining about. If your TV is in the same room as your drawers, this is a no brainer. I have been known to remove the drawers from a dresser, one at a time, and take them into the room where I was watching TV. During the commercial break, I switch drawers.

- Sort through your magazine rack, tossing out the *House Beautiful* magazines from 1985—trust me, all the rooms that you thought "were you" in 1985 are now someone else.

- Do some ironing.

- Polish the silver that you have on display, but only if it is tarnished.

- Put those recipes that you jotted down on pieces of scrap paper into a basket or box near your other cookbooks. They won't get misplaced, and they'll all be together for when you choose to:

- Transcribe them onto 3" x 5" cards, put them into a manila file folder, or slip them into plastic sleeves that snap into a loose leaf notebook.

QUICK ⬭ PAINLESS

Take a drawer and a garbage bag into the TV room. I wouldn't be surprised if in 60 minutes (or during) you can clean out your entire dresser or all the junk drawers in your kitchen.

If you don't make cleaning a big deal, your kids won't think it is either. By letting them know that tidying up is part of the activity that they are already doing (and part of life, but maybe wait until they're older to emphasize that), your kids won't feel like it's punishment, and may actually start cleaning up without being told to!

CALL IN THE TROOPS

Wives, husbands, children, partners, and others—everyone who lives under the same roof, are part of your cleaning team. Your cleaning team is an equal opportunity employer; there is no preference given to age or sex. And cooperation is the key.

Kids Can Do the Darndest Things

I certainly don't want to come across sounding like a child psychologist, but children need to develop into responsible adults. When is the best time to start teaching them to be accountable? As soon as possible, as far as I'm concerned.

Here are a few tips to start the ball rolling. (Check out the chapters on the kitchen, bathroom, and children's rooms for additional kids' participation tips.)

- Teach your toddler to put her toys into the toy box. When my kids were little, Cookie Monster and Big Bird were the mentors to the little munchkins. Today, it's Barney. If you incorporate the songs and lessons that your children learn from their television buddies while they learn to pick up their toys, the job will get done with smiles.

- Teach your five-year old how to make his bed. Convince him that this is one of life's passages from little-boyhood to big-boyhood. It does not matter what the quality of the final job is; it was terrific in your eyes and he has every right to brag about it to his friends.

- It's never too early to have the kids throw their dirty clothes into a laundry basket or down the laundry chute.

- You're really in luck if your home was built with a laundry chute. The excitement of tossing dirty clothes into a hole in the wall, where they mysteriously disappear (remember, your kids aren't doing the laundry, yet) takes several years to wear off. You really need to put your foot down, however, when it comes to throwing the youngest kid down the chute because his clothes are soiled. (Please note: An unabridged dictionary and a half set of encyclopedias will dislodge anything that is wedged in the chute channel.)

- Have the kids set and clear the table. When they are really little, you may only want them to clear their own place setting. (This can take some time. Little hands can't hold much. You may prefer them to start with their plate, then their glass, and then their silverware.) If everyone in the family helps, the kitchen will be cleaned up in half the time, and then you can go out for ice cream!

- You do the laundry, but let the kids put their own underwear away. Sharing the tasks will speed up the end result. (Don't worry what the drawers look like—you'll show them how to keep their dresser drawers in order before they go to college.)

IF YOU'RE SO INCLINED

There are some really interesting laundry bins made for young people. If your child wants to be the next Michael, or Michelle, Jordan, find one that looks like a basketball hoop. There are many stores that do custom design work and can create something appealing for the ballerina, astronaut, or racecar driver.

Husbandry is More Than Agriculture

I know. It is unfair to pick on the man of the house. But, let's face it: History and nature charged women with caring for home and hearth. But, thank heaven, times have changed. Women spouses hold full-time jobs, and male spouses chip in with the household chores. Here are a few tips to encourage history not to repeat itself.

- Sit down with your spouse or significant other and choose which chores each of you enjoys doing, or at least doesn't mind doing.

- Let go of the masculine/feminine household job stereotypes. If one of you enjoys cooking, then the other can clean up.

- Become a dream team. My husband has sharing responsibilities down to a science. He has decided that I get pleasure from his having crisply starched shirts and wrinkle-free clothing. Therefore, he has given me the enjoyable task of sending his shirts to the laundry, and he does not complain when I press the wrinkles out of his suits. I, in turn, keep him in line by offering to starch his underwear.

- You might decide that laundry is a job that you want to take turns doing.

- And garbage is a task that will give the children strength of character.

What we're after is teamwork and the fastest and easiest way to achieve an acceptable level of spotlessness!

This chapter has gone pretty well, don't you think? But I don't want you to overdo it. As the song says, "We've only just begun." I think that you should reward yourself for your efforts. Go out and do Double Duty! That's one triple-dip ice cream cone for each hand.

The Lazy Way

Getting Time on Your Side

	The Old Way	**The Lazy Way**
Cleaning up a big meal	30 minutes	10 minutes
Making the beds	15 minutes	5 minutes
Doing laundry	2 hours	1 hour
Polishing silver	45 minutes	25 minutes
Sorting the mail	5 minutes	2 minutes
Cleaning out a drawer	20 minutes	10 minutes

Chapter five

Keep It Clean Without Becoming the Maid

Have you heard the story about the homemaker that spent all day straightening her house in preparation for the maid's coming the next day to clean? I find that story ridiculous, but not just because someone is cleaning the house in preparation to get the house cleaned, but also because there is no way that I would want to spend an entire day cleaning. I like my surroundings to be neat all the time. I don't like dirt, and, yes, I am the type of person who worries about what my friends think. (I'm trying to get over this, but I don't have the time right now for extensive therapy.) I'm sure, like me, there are so many other things besides cleaning that you'd rather be doing, or need to be doing.

At some point in time, all of us have to put our homes in order, both literally and figuratively. You want to keep your abode clean and tidy, but not at the expense of taking too much time away from your family, and things you want to, or have to do. Well, once you've taken a little time to organize your housecleaning it will practically take care of itself.

I don't know about you, but I find that putting order into my life relieves stress. Order gives me more time to relax, lets me know what I have to face next, and prepares me to meet it head on. Order eliminates searching, extra steps, doing it twice, and straightening up for company. I've learned how to clean house and do a good job at it without making a career of it. I have a home I'm comfortable in and proud of, and I have plenty of time to do other things. If you've been falling short in your housecleaning and feeling frustrated about it, think of this book as a stress reliever!

My husband and I are now empty nesters. I work full time; he and I travel often for both business and pleasure. We each have a variety of outside interests. Yes, in some respects, our lifestyle makes it easier to maintain orderliness. In other respects, it's still the "same old, same old." For example, instead of my daughter coming home with her sweaty field hockey uniform and dirty cleats, my husband brings a whole team's worth of pungent basketball jerseys into the house. (He sponsors teams, as well as plays in tournaments.) And often he is so exhausted that he leaves them in a pile at the back door, or on the basement floor near the washing machine.

And while it may not be my son tracking in mud after playing touch football in the backyard anymore, it's the mud from the woods. We have a cottage in the country where we like to spend relaxing weekends. It's *au naturel* out there, meaning there's lots of mud and no washing machine. We come home from our treks with our boots and clothes covered in dirt, which ends up on the floor at home. Great end to a relaxing weekend, huh?

And we can't forget the:

- Husband, who may be very neat, but is also very busy. His cleaning spurts are not scheduled. When not in a spurt mood, he is in a "leave it in a heap" mode.

- And then of course there's the black cat named Inky, the visiting golden retriever named Crosier, and the Iguana named Maui.

- Last but not least, there are our five children (as well as all of the stuff they can't fit in their apartments).

Needless to say, this house has all kinds of opportunities to get dirty. But without my spending hours cleaning, my home is always ready for unexpected guests. How do I accomplish this, you ask? Well, read on.

GET IN THE HABIT OF GETTING RID OF THE JUNK

Have you ever noticed that a little dust on a tabletop goes unnoticed, but three weeks worth of mail sitting in that dust attracts attention? It's not the dust so much that makes your house look dirty and unkempt, it's the stuff that you have lying around in the dust. The first step to creating neat surroundings is to discard the junk. The second step is to stop collecting it. That is, adopt the habit of regularly getting rid of items that are not really contributing to a blissful existence.

YOU'LL THANK YOURSELF LATER

Don't let your home resemble Fibber McGee's closet. Don't save a broken item to use as spare parts. That's what hardware stores are all about— spare parts.

If you're a yard sale fanatic, you're probably thinking that one man's junk is another man's treasure. Agreed. But it's only a treasure if it's useable, appealing to the eye, or has some special value only to you. Then, it should have a place to call its own. Anything else that just sits around the house collecting dust is, in one word—junk. I bet if you open those "mystery" boxes in the basement, you'll probably find junk. Get rid of it!

If you are a saver, you probably have many pieces that are common rat pack items. Here are a few tips on how to simplify what to save and what not to save.

Recycle Your Clothes

Clothing styles are cyclical; A "look" may come back into fashion. But the designers are not dummies. Do you think that they're going to put a full-page ad in *Vogue* telling you to pull out your psychedelic colored bell-bottoms because they're back in style? Clothing designers and manufacturers are out to make a buck. Psychedelic colors might hit the runway this spring. Bell-bottoms might come back into fashion. But psychedelic bell-bottoms probably won't. And if, by chance, there were such an animal (heaven forbid), the purveyors of fashion would be sure to create ever-so-slight subtleties, guaranteeing that the psychedelic colored bell-bottoms you've saved for these past 20 years will look as though you have saved them these past 20 years.

One of my friends told me that she was taking some of her old clothes to a consignment shop. If they sold, she got some cash, if they didn't, they were donated to a charity. Since I love the idea of extra dough in my wallet, I thought I'd try it out. That following weekend, I went down to the basement and dragged up all of the clothes that I had been storing there (waiting for them to come back into style). I packed them into my car and took them to the consignment shop. (In my mind, I was already spending my newfound cash.)

But instead of money, all I received was rejection. My clothes were too old to be sold! They were out of style. No one would buy them. Then what was I saving them for? Good question.

Here are a few tips for recycling your clothes through a consignment shop:

- Call the shop to check the specific criteria for bringing in old clothes.

- Ask what percentage of the selling price you will receive.

- Ask what happens to the clothes if they do not sell within a specific amount of time.

- Many shops handle only women's clothing. Ask if they carry men's and children's merchandise. If they don't, ask if they know who does.

- Ask what their age requirements are (for the clothes, not you). Most consignment stores require that clothing be no more than two years old.

- Most consignment stores require that the clothes be clean and free of stains and tears.

YOU'LL THANK YOURSELF LATER

This is my own personal mantra. If you wore it in the 1960s you shouldn't wear it in the 1990s (and NEVER in the year 2000!).

IF YOU'RE SO

INCLINED

If you become an empty nester, try to reclaim your valuable storage space. Invite your children to visit you for the weekend. Walk down memory lane together, reminisce about childhood mementos, and then insist that the adult darlings take the stuff with them, or throw it out.

- Most consignment stores tell you to bring in your clothes on hangers.
- Many consignment stores specify certain days of the week on which they will accept merchandise. Be sure to ask, so that you don't waste a trip.

"Thanks for the Memories"

When storage space is at a premium, you have to look hard and long at memorabilia. Is this an item that really holds strong sentimental attachment for you? Once you decide to keep an object, you have to continually justify its presence because of the valuable space it takes up (not to mention the dust it collects).

If you're no longer using something, then why are you saving it? Like your old clothes, it's probably outdated. If it's not, then it's most likely to be:

- Ugly.
- Something you can't believe you bought and can't remember why.
- A gift from Aunt Dora that you didn't like when you opened the box but felt too guilty to return.
- Just plain broken—you plan on using the pieces for spare parts.
- Triplicates, quadruplicates et al. You do not have to keep three, five, or 10 of an item "just in case."

Items like these are not going to become more valuable sitting around. All they are is clutter, dust collectors, and garbage waiting to happen. Don't dwell on them. Get rid of them!

Okay. If you bit the bullet, you divided the piles into "yes," "no," and "maybe." (Let's hope that "maybe" isn't the largest pile.) Sort things this way once or twice a year and you'll find the "maybe" stuff moving effortlessly to the "no" pile. What do you do with all the stuff that you have decided to get rid of? Donate it.

Many charities welcome the donation of household items and old clothes. Again, you cannot assume that all agencies are willing to accept every kind of merchandise. I suggest that you call first, so that you know the criteria for making donations.

Call the Garbage Truck

You may be surprised to discover that your treasures are not even suitable as a donation. I know that you may have great sentimental attachment to that swag lamp from your old college dorm room, but will you ever use it? Would anybody else? If we're talking garbage, a phone call to your local garbage company can save you time and aggravation. Here are some questions that you may want to ask:

- Will they pick up the kind of item(s) you are throwing out?
- Do the items have to be packaged in any particular way?
- When do they pick up these types of items?

Just imagine how much space you could create, effortlessly, just by making sensible choices about what to keep part of your housecleaning routine.

QUICK ⟨n⟩ PAINLESS

Are you acquainted with the phrase "regifting"? Regifting is giving items that you have received (but that do not suit your lifestyle) to others who you think might really appreciate them.

MAINTAIN WITHOUT PAIN

I know that no one is going to redecorate her home simply to try to cut down on cleaning, but here are some tips to keep in mind if you do decide to buy something new or for when it is time to redo. Some kinds of furnishings and floors are easier to take care of than others.

Flooring

Have you ever heard that when you design a room you should start from the bottom and work up? Well, that's what the decorators tell me. There are so many interesting and wonderful floorings from which to choose. Pick one that you love and at the same time find easy to keep up. Because if it takes you forever to clean your floor, you'll fall out of love with it.

When you look into flooring:

- Choose floor coverings that are relatively easy to keep clean.

- Ask about the finish on linoleum flooring. Does it keep its shine, or do you have to clean it often and with special products?

- Hardwood floors are also very popular and do not need the upkeep that they did in times gone by. There have been great strides made with hardwood floors. A polyurethane finish retains the beauty of the wood without the hassle and seems to lessen dirt build-up. Water beads right off, spills wipe up with a paper towel, and a mop gets rid of the dust bunnies.

IF YOU'RE SO INCLINED

Some donations may be tax deductible. Speak to your accountant or tax preparer for details. Keep a list of all the items you donate and get a receipt from the institution to which you made the donation.

- Everyone I know who has a tile floor, especially white, loves the way the floor looks, but says that it takes a lot of work to keep it clean. The job really becomes time consuming if you have dogs and children. The upside of tile is that you can wipe them up with a wet mop or towel.

- There are newer wood look-alike laminates, like Pergo or Wilsoncraft. They are easier to maintain than real wood, and look nicer than vinyl.

There's a vast range of carpeting, and some of the factors to consider are:

Color

Dark-colored carpeting may not show dirt as readily as light-colored carpeting, but dark carpets show more lint than light carpets do.

Style

Carpeting styles, like styles of furniture, are very personal. It's all a matter of what you find to be appealing. You may decide to create a different atmosphere in each room, with a different style of rug, such as:

- **Plush:** I think that this carpet looks the way the word sounds. It has a very smooth finish and can be of varied thickness or pile. Plush carpeting, no matter what color, shows footprints. In my home, I have a plush carpet in the living room, on the stairs, and in the upstairs hall. It is very thick, has a great pad, and shows every footstep. So, if you feel this is going to bother you, check out the next type.

YOU'LL THANK YOURSELF LATER

Put newspaper or a paper towel under your pet's food and water bowls. When your Doberman dribbles on the floor, roll up the paper, food, water, and all, and toss it into the trash.

If you've carpeted your living room wall to wall in a color that won't show much dirt and grime, ask your carpet layer to bind a piece of the remnant and use it at your front door. You'll be able to vacuum and spot clean the doormat the same way you vacuum your carpet.

Commercial carpeting: Commercial carpeting has come a long way since its inception. Those of us who "went contemporary" in the 1970s had this type of carpet in several rooms of our home. I've had the same commercial carpet in our family room for at least 15 years. It is a very good grade and is still wearing like iron. This carpet is flat and thick and has virtually no pile (à la no footprints). A nice thick pad can add bounce and protect the underside of the rug from wearing out. Some commercial carpets have rubber backing. (I've been told that the rubber backing tends to disintegrate with wear, and spills have a tendency to sink into the rubber and remain for long periods of time.)

We also have another variety of commercial carpeting that is glued to the floor of the finished room in our basement. It comes nowhere near the quality of the carpet in the family room, but withstood a horrific flood that left the basement filled with eight feet of water. All we had to do, after bailing and drying out, was to clean it. It looks as good as it did the day we had it laid.

Patterned Carpet: Patterned carpet can be really attractive. The pattern may be of one hue, tone-on-tone, or a variety of colors. I find that I get so interested in the intricacies of the design, I tend not to see lint, footprints, or dirt.

Shag: Shag carpeting was very popular in the Sixties and Seventies. I haven't seen much around, of late. Real shag aficionados owned a rake that they used after vacuuming and that brought up the nap of the carpet.

Furniture Facts

There are so many beautiful styles of furniture. You're the one that is going to live with it, so be sure to choose something that is appealing and makes you feel good about your surroundings. Of course, there will be care and maintenance of any kind of furniture, and an important part of keeping house is in what goes on the furniture, not the furniture, itself.

 If you do go furniture shopping, and are looking for expediency in cleaning, as well as style and design, here are a few tips to keep in mind:

- Wood and veneers need a flick of a feather to take care of the dust that inevitably settles. Furniture polish, from time to time, is something you will want to apply for that added shine. But relax, and don't overdo the polish; it's shine that you're looking for, not wax build-up. Consider a polyurethane finish on some of your wood furniture. Water will bead up, you'll be able to wipe it off with a sponge, and window cleaner will remove harder-to-clean stains. I, personally, would not put polyurethane on finer pieces of furniture or antiques, but you may wish to check with your furniture store or antique dealer.

- Glass is really easy to keep clean. All you need is a bottle of window cleaner and a roll of paper towels. The only thing that may distort the look of glass is a scratch or chip here and there. Just think of it as

YOU'LL THANK YOURSELF LATER

Don't use furniture polish every time you clean a piece of furniture. Using polish every time you dust adds a wax build up (as the commercial says). Wax is grease, and grease draws dust like a magnet.

character. Don't let it bother you. Imperfections can always be buffed out or the entire piece can be replaced. The benefit of glass is that stains and spills wash right off.

■ Formica furniture is also a cinch to keep up. Again, I just use window cleaner and paper towels. I have a white Formica table that I have been known to use a little Soft Scrub on to remove a stubborn stain.

Don't Freak Over Fabric

I learned my lesson the hard way when it comes to choosing fabric for furniture. I'll let you learn yours the easy way:

■ **Scotch Gard:** I definitely lean toward darker colors that have been Scotch Garded at the factory. The biggest mistake that I made when decorating my home was choosing a light taupe fabric for our family room sofa. I was sure that I had all my bases covered. I had the sofas upholstered with fabric that was protected with Scotch Gard; I made sure that there were both glass and Formica tables where the children could eat, drink, draw, and play games. I just didn't know about two little items, which have ruined the look of this mammoth L-shaped divan:

1. The fabric could not be cleaned with anything that was water-soluble. Therefore, the soil protector was not as useful as I had thought it would be. It stained from water spots.

2. When I read the newspaper, I rest it on the couch. Newspaper print leaves a slightly darkened cast to fabric. The ink really shows on taupe fabric and does not come out, even when cleaned professionally.

- **Patterns and Prints:** Stains will get lost in patterns, dark prints, and stripes.

- **Versatile Cushions:** Be sure that your cushions are made so that they can be flipped every few weeks or when mishaps occur.

- **Throw Pillows:** Use throw pillows of various sizes and designs not only to embellish your décor, but also to hide myriad spots, stains, and general schmutz.

Stage a Knickknack Attack

The more collectibles you display, the more knickknacks on the shelves, the more pictures on view, the more dust there is to deal with. Ergo, the more time you spend doing housework. If you feel guilty for not dusting often enough, but don't want to spend the time, face the prospect of living with fewer little things around to dust. If you want to clean up your act:

- Unload the bookshelves of figurines and extraneous collectibles. Choose just a few that you wish to display.

- Ask your grown children if they would like the ones that you have tired of. Or "regift" those that you do not wish to use. Donate those that no one wants to a thrift shop.

QUICK **n** *PAINLESS*

Club soda is a great stain remover for non-greasy spills, especially red wine. Doesn't the waiter always run to get you some soda after he spills the wine on your new outfit?

Straighten up your coffee table. Make the tabletops safe for high-speed housework. Limit the number of pieces that you have to move and clean under.

That doesn't mean that you'll never exhibit the picture of the 11-point buck or the fish that got away. Just don't have all of your treasures on display at the same time. Rotate them. And when they are not in full view, hide them.

Hidden Treasures

"Oh, where, oh, where has my little dog gone. Oh, where, oh where, can he be?" Try looking next to the fireplace in the persimmon Shaker box with the homespun decal on the cover.

There are a plethora of baskets, boxes, and drawers that can be used for decorative storage. They can sit on top of tables, under tables, or on shelves. They can be nested or perched. Their charm is that they keep your belongings organized and at your fingertips, while at the same time helping you expedite cleaning chores. Once you have these containers in place, and get into the habit of placing the respective items inside them, you're already eliminating a whole step of cleaning—removing the clutter.

Survey your room. Is the mail piled on the end table? Are a year's worth of magazines sitting on the cocktail table? Is the sweater that you've been knitting since 1985 perched on the arm of the sofa (along with knitting needles and three skeins of wool)? Picture what your room

would look like without these items in clear view. Neat, huh. Looks like the maid came in this morning, doesn't it?

Here are some suggestions of what to do with the daily "stuff" we all seem to accumulate (which then accumulates dust).

- Stack magazines in a basket and place it under a hall table or in a bathroom.
- Keep your pencils, pens, and notepads in a covered box near the telephone.
- Store your three pairs of grocery store reading glasses in little holders near each telephone, and where you sort the mail.
- Keep paper clips, rubber bands, stapler, and staples in small baskets on your writing desk or wherever you sit down to pay your bills.

Better Once Than Twice

Articles on time management tell you not to handle a piece of paper more than once. When you open your mail at work, you simply read and reply. Then the task is over. The same premise can save you time and energy at home. Do it right the first time. You're eventually going to have to pick the things up, anyway. Why not put them away now and avoid creating a future chore? Better once than twice.

Follow some of these tips and you'll save yourself time, energy, and headaches later on:

- Put dirty dishes directly into the dishwasher. It takes as much energy to put a dish into the sink as it does to put it into the dishwasher.

QUICK **n** *PAINLESS*

You do not even have to leave your home to shop for receptacles that are both decorative and practical. Catalogs, such as for Hold Everything, are full of the most creative items that serve this purpose. Order a few catalogs and enjoy looking through them comfortably, in the very room you're buying the items for.

- And when you unload the dishwasher, empty its contents directly into the cupboards and drawers where they belong. Try to avoid leaving things on the countertops to be put away later. Mañana never comes.

- Don't leave your dirty clothes next to the hamper; open the lid and put them inside. (And, if you haven't already noticed, the dishwasher and the hamper are both closed containers. Out of sight, out of mind.)

- Hang or put your car keys in the same place each time you come home. Then you won't have to run around like a chicken without a head, blaming everyone and everything in sight for taking them.

- Place a little cabinet near the door that you most often enter and exit, garage or front, depending upon how you travel. Designate this cabinet as the spot where:

1. You leave your keys, your briefcase, the letter that you have to mail tomorrow.

2. You leave your grocery list for the items that you must pick up after work tomorrow.

3. You leave the phone number of your son's third grade classroom teacher. You have to call her tomorrow to explain that the rare skin ailment you have suddenly contracted prohibits you from baking the 12 dozen cookies for the soccer team's fund-raiser on Thursday.

4. You put the kids' lunches and milk money. You may decide to use a drawer of this cabinet to store rolls of quarters so that you always have milk money.

5. You deposit anything that you have to remember to take with you when you leave the house in the morning.

And once you earmark this cabinet to be the keeper of the keys, briefcase, milk money, and the "to do tomorrow" list, you stick to it. I guarantee that your life will be a little easier, a lot neater, and you will always know where to find your keys.

A job well done! Now take the old photos that you found in the basement, go into the family room, put your feet up, and reminisce of time and pounds gone by. (Was that you with a full head of hair?)

The Lazy Way

Getting Time on Your Side

	The Old Way	**The Lazy Way**
Finding your car keys	5 minutes	0 minutes
Putting clean dishes away	10 minutes	5 minutes
Gathering dirty clothes to be washed	6 minutes	1 minute
Dusting the coffee table	3 minutes	1 minute
Removing stains from the couch	30 minutes	5 minutes

Home Clean Home: Speedy Spotlessness

Are You Too Lazy to Read Speedy Spotlessness?

1 Your home was selected as the number one project in a "Save the Neighborhood" clean-up campaign. ☐ yes ☐ no

2 Several friends congratulated you upon hearing that you were one of the fastest-growing Web sites (as in spider web). ☐ yes ☐ no

3 After seeing the condition of your house, burglars make a hasty exit. ☐ yes ☐ no

Hallowed Halls in Half the Time

You may have a front hall, and it may be small or spacious, one-story or two, grand in its style or homey in décor. Or your front door may open straight into your living room. Whichever it is, the space just inside the door is the first thing that anyone sees when they come to call. By following the tips in Chapter 5, "Keep It Clean," you can create a space that is attractive, practical, welcoming, but most of all a cinch to keep orderly.

Survey the area near the door. Well, it could be lovely—if it weren't such a magnet for clutter.

SORT IT OUT

There's stuff piled everywhere: coats, scarves, mail, shoes, things that need to be taken upstairs, your pink monogrammed bowling ball that your neighbor borrowed for a Sixties costume party and returned to you a month ago, and various and sundry items that have to do with day-to-day living. Now, don't fret. We'll walk through this and, in no time, deal with it.

Survey Your Stuff

Your front hall can store a plethora of mismatched belongings ranging from:

- Bar items
- Sporting goods
- Holiday paraphernalia
- Camera equipment
- Fabric and wallpaper remnants
- Halloween costumes
- Cookbooks

It's all in how you hide it, store it, and keep it out of the way. It's how you make less mess.

Let's clear everything off the table, the floor, and the chair and sort it all out. What do we have here?

- Mail: bills, invitations, correspondence, and the trusty junk
- Magazines
- Shoes and boots
- Gloves
- Scarves
- Coats and jackets
- Book bags
- Briefcase

IF YOU'RE SO
INCLINED

If your taste leans toward antiques, you can create more storage space in your hallway by investing in a Victorian-styled hall chair. The chair is high-backed and decorated with a mirror and clothing hooks. The seat is hinged and, when raised, has the perfect compartment to store gloves and scarves. Many of these chairs have attached compartments for umbrellas as well.

- Workout clothes (Double whew!! They're ripening as we speak.)
- Plants
- Family pictures
- Your antique doorknob collection
- The pink monogrammed bowling ball (Whatever happened to the matching bowling bag?)

First, sort everything into "yes," "no," and "maybe" piles. Get rid of the "No's" immediately. Already there's less to deal with! Then sort by destination: laundry, back to your neighbor, bedrooms, basement, etc. What you'll have left is what belongs near the door—on a hook, on a table, in a basket, or in the closet.

Most of the closets in your home are private niches where your treasures hide, far from any criticizing eyes. All except the closet in your front hall. That multipurpose cupboard known as the "guest" closet is open for viewing to complete strangers.

Closet Cleanout

Let's start by taking a look in the closet. Oh, boy! We have a little organizing to do. First, take out the clothes that you picked up at the cleaners. Put them aside. We'll cover them in the chapter on bedroom closets. The next area to tackle is the closet shelf. If it is in complete disarray, you'll have to clean everything off and sort it into piles. (Refer to Chapter 5.) My guess is that there are a few items that you don't have any use for anymore. Sort your treasures into "yes," "no," and "maybe."

A COMPLETE WASTE OF TIME

The Three Worst Things to Save:

1. Single gloves; you're not going to find the one that you lost.

2. The gold and black-striped, 10-foot-long muffler that just isn't going to cut it any more. (Unless, of course, you're a Pittsburgh Steeler's fan. If you're not, find someone who is and bestow it on him as a gift.)

3. The ski hat you wore as a child—you know, the one with the frog embroidered on the side and pompom on top.

IF YOU'RE SO
INCLINED

If there is unused space between the top of the items that you store in your front hall closet and the ceiling, you may wish to consider adding another shelf to keep rarely utilized minutiae.

STORE IT

Now that you've got your goods in order, it's time to get them out of sight. For many of us, the front hall or coat closet has to store more than coats. This is where a little creativity comes in handy.

Creative Closets

In my house, the front hall closet is the only place that I can hide the leaves to my glass-and-chrome dining room table. Besides the fact that tossing non-outerware items into the closet can become messy and disorganized, I also needed to safely and conveniently store the extenders, so I didn't have to worry about the glass breaking as someone hurries to grab her coat before she misses the school bus. Therefore, I had a press-board storage bin built and had it attached to the back wall of the closet. It not only protects the glass leaves, but also stores them in an upright position and facilitates taking them in and out of the closet. If you find that you have large items like this, you may want to consider having something "built in." This does not have to be a do-it-yourself project. A good handyman can put something like my storage area together in an hour or two for very little money. A furniture store or an interior decorator may know someone who can carry out these kinds of projects.

Besides being safe storage, something you have built in can also divide the closet to create a more organized space. For example, this table-leaf bin divides my front closet into two sections. I hang coats and jackets in the larger space to the right of the bin and use the smaller space on the left to hang tablecloths. I put the matching napkins in baskets on the shelf, above.

Coats

Common sense, and our mothers, tell us that coats belong in the closet and not thrown over the back of a chair, hung on the banister, or, heaven forbid, tossed onto the floor. As someone's mother, I feel a responsibility to review with you what needs to be done with your outerwear when you are no longer out.

Look at the previous list. Coats are an easy choice to go into the closet first. After all, the front hall closet is what is known in some homes as the coat closet.

Hanging Up the Coats

To keep the hall (and the rest of the house) free of coats and jackets, follow these simple steps. You'll need:

- Hangers

1 Hang up each of your coats on its own hanger. Doubling up is not allowed.

2 The thin wire hangers that you get from the cleaners just won't cut it for your heavy outerwear. Invest in hangers made of thick plastic or wood that will support your coats and jackets without drooping under the weight.

IF YOU'RE SO
INCLINED

Your closet will be more eye appealing if all of the hangers match. Check out closet specialty stores for the widest array of styles and prices. If you really want style, wooden monogrammed hangers are very chic.

Hats and Gloves

Now you have room to organize the remainder of your
hats, gloves, scarves, earmuffs, headbands, and other
winter paraphernalia. You'll need:

- Decorative baskets or colorful plastic bins
- Hooks for the back of the closet door. (Unless your
  closet has tracked sliding doors; you may then wish
  to hang extra hooks on the inside sidewalls.)
- Mesh or clear plastic tote bag

1. Place gloves in pairs along with scarves and hats into baskets or bins. If you live in a real he-man winter climate, like
   I do, you may want one basket for gloves and another one
   for scarves.

If you're using hooks on the back of the door:

1. Hang your scarves and hats on the pegs, trying to place
   one item per peg.

2. Place gloves in their pairs in the tote bag and hang the
   bag on one of the pegs.

Rein in Those Umbrellas

Okay. All of your outerwear is neatly hung up, and your
scarves and gloves are put away. What's left piled on
the floor of the closet? Umbrellas. You'll need any of the
following:

- Shelf
- Umbrella stand
- Hooks

1 Line up the collapsible umbrellas on the shelf.

2 Put the full-sized umbrellas into an attractive umbrella stand or large jardinière near the front door.

3 Hang any umbrellas that have a strap from the accordion-pegged device on the back of the door or a hook attached to the inside wall.

Shoes and Boots

My kids, and even I, sometimes, kick off our shoes when we walk into the house. This is a good thing, because the carpets stay cleaner. This is a bad thing if there are stray shoes and boots left sitting in the front hall.

Here are a few solutions to avoid the shoe scramble:

1. Place a big basket next to the door where everyone can deposit their footwear. It lacks in formality, but who cares? You can remove it when having a formal get together if it really bothers you. It not only keeps the entranceway looking tidy, but also prevents tripping over misplaced sneakers every time you walk in the door.

2. Put a plastic laundry basket inside the garage near the door to the house. If you live in tundra country, the way I do, it's a real time saver to let sloppy, salty boots drip onto the garage floor rather than permitting them to form a puddle in your back hall.

YOU'LL THANK YOURSELF LATER

When you purchase hooks to hang behind your closet door, check into one of the simplest types. It is made of wood and, when opened, accordions out into diamond shapes that have pegs on each point. The device can be adjusted to fit onto a large or small area of the door, and, because of its configuration, it will hang a large number of items.

Managing the Mail

If the entranceway is a convenient place to sort your mail, you should create decorative storage places for it—everything from bills to letters to catalogs and newspapers.

Some attractive alternatives are:

1. **Baskets:** I love baskets. I use them for many different purposes. You can find some great ones with covers to use to store the mail.

2. **Covered boxes:** This is where you can let your creativity and style shine, since there is such a variety. Here are just a few you might want to consider:

   - Old hat boxes of various sizes can be very interesting. Stack them in descending size from the floor up. Keep your mail in the one on top.

   - Hand-crafted wooden boxes made from various types of wood. Some even come inlaid with beautiful designs in diverse colors.

   - Old covered boxes that you find at flea markets or yard sales. Clean them up a little, keep them looking old with their natural patina, or paint them bright colors to match your décor.

   - Unfinished Shaker-type boxes that you find in art supply stores. I think that they look great *au naturel*, but decorating them may start you on a road to a new hobby. Or, have the kids bedeck them.

QUICK 🔲 PAINLESS

For a simple way to store paperwork while adding color and style to the room, purchase a few photograph storage boxes. Nowadays, you can find them in a variety of colors and patterns. They're easy to stack and don't take up a lot of room. And don't toss the organizing cards that came with them; although the file cards are meant to create order out of your photos, there's no reason you can't use them to manage your mail.

3. **Tins:** they're not just for cookies anymore. Tins come in all price ranges, sizes, and designs. Many old tins have become collectibles. Use a different tin for different seasons or holidays of the year: Thanksgiving, spring, Fourth of July. Be creative and have fun while you get your mail and your act together!

Take Control of Your Correspondence

Mail clutter can be divided into four categories. You'll need:

- closed containers (see previous suggestions)
- basket
- garbage can
- recycling bin

1 As you sort through your mail, divide it into the following piles:

- Authentic mail clutter or "keepers" (bills, invitations, birthday cards)
- Unwanted mail clutter or "read it, keep it, or toss it (notice of sales, coupons, the annual block party flyer)
- Junk mail (no explanation necessary)
- Magazines and catalogs

IF YOU'RE SO INCLINED

A reader of *Better Homes and Gardens* suggested how to cut down on the volumes of catalogs that pile up in your home. Tear out the pages that feature the item that you plan to purchase, or want to add to your wish list. Be sure that that the page has the catalog's phone number on it or else that you jot down the order phone number and the name of the catalog on the sheet. Put the pages into a file folder or manila envelope for easier keeping.

2 Put the bills and items that you wish to keep into the closed containers that you've designated for these items.

3 Place magazines and catalogs underneath a table or in a bare corner. Pile them up on the floor horizontally, or nestle them in baskets.

4 Throw everything that is junk mail and everything that you've read and don't want to keep into the garbage. In many communities, magazines and catalogs go into the recycling bin.

GARBAGE CAN CONTROVERSIES

My husband believes that, for quicker dumping, all garbage cans should be lined with garbage bags. Granted, that would speed up the collection process. However, I believe that the only garbage cans that deserve to be lined with plastic garbage bags are the ones in the kitchen, basement, and garage.

All the other trash cans in our house took me months to find. They are not just receptacles for rubbish; they are "part of the décor that makes a house a home."

I'm sure that there are many households like ours. To bag, or not to bag, that is the question. Try these compromises on for size:

- Find a decorative basket with an attractive lid to use for trash where you sort the mail.
- Line a small wastebasket with a small plastic garbage bag, and then hide the wastebasket in a lower cupboard.

QUICK n' PAINLESS

If you want to protect the magazines from collecting any dust, at all, purchase a series of closed baskets or boxes of various sizes. Fill with magazines and stack one on top of the other, creatively, under the hall table.

- Hide small bags (the size of car litterbags) in one of the hatboxes, wooden boxes or tins that you have nesting in the front hall. When you sort through the mail, toss the junk into a litterbag and throw that bag into the kitchen trash can.

SUCCINCT SOLUTIONS TO SLOPPY STAIRCASES

What do halls, entranceways, and staircases have in common? They're magnets for everything that's brought into your home and not immediately put away. Staircases have an interesting way of becoming coat hooks and dry cleaning hangers as well as a multi-leveled organizer for various piles of stuff that needs to go upstairs.

If you own an older home, or if you have built your home and have incorporated some of those wonderful gracious elements from days gone by, you may be one of the lucky individuals who possess a back staircase. These staircases usually originate in the kitchen or back hall. They are within the inner sanctum of the family, and are, therefore, private and personal. Schoolbooks, briefcases, and the other paraphernalia sitting on a back staircase are there because they "lie in wait until needed."

Most of us, however, have only one staircase, which is generally smack dab in the front of the house, and the first thing you see when you walk in the front door. Schoolbooks, briefcases, and the other paraphernalia sitting on a front staircase create an obstacle course and look messy.

QUICK n' PAINLESS

Deposit all the items that need to go upstairs into a hamper at the foot of the stairs. The first person to make a trip upstairs takes the basket with him or her. You may even want another basket at the top of the stairs that serves the reverse purpose.

IF YOU'RE SO
INCLINED

If you have a table or floor lamp in the hallway, spray the light bulbs with purfume, aftershave, or potpourri spray. Every time you turn on the light, the heat will distribute the aroma around the room. What a way to welcome guests!

The answer to this staircase catastrophe is simple: Hide the items in a decorative closed container that is easy to carry. May I suggest something along the lines of a picnic basket with a hinged lid? The attached cover won't get misplaced, and isn't a pain to take off and put on. The handles are comfortable to grab, and the basket can manage a good deal of weight.

HIDDEN TREASURES

Now, for your door knob collection. They are really beautiful, but the brass is tarnished, and they're covered with a lot of grease and dust. What luck! That movie you've been waiting to see is on television tonight. Grab your door knobs and the brass polish and Double Duty this job. (See Chapter 4, "Sweep It Under the Rug.")

Nice job. Those babies really do shine. What are you going to do with them now? If you put them back on top of the table, they'll just collect dust, again.

Here's a solution: enclose them in a Lucite box and hang the assortment above the hall table. Your doorknobs are displayed for everyone to admire, you've added charm to the front hall décor, and you probably won't have to polish the ensemble for a long time.

What to do with your birdhouse collection? Install a shelf about a foot from the ceiling to display the hummingbird homes. Be sure to leave room for additions to your collection.

Do you own wonderful old family photos that you would like to exhibit? Fill an entire wall with the pictures that you have similarly matted and framed.

If your hall has a window, what about increasing the depth of the sill or installing shelves across the window itself to hold your African violets or orchids? For a more interesting impact, use flowerpots that are similar in style and color. Or if you own a set of antique cachepots, why not fill them with simple green plants?

KEEP IT CLEAN

Wow! Now that all that stuff is gone, you can actually see the floor and top of the table. (And you can also see the dirt and dust!) Here are tips that will help you to clean in a flash!

Footloose and Fancy Free Furniture

Hallways vary in size, shape, and décor. One entranceway may have a mammoth piece of furniture, while others hold nothing more than a single chair, or a bench, or a small side table. And then there are hallways with no furniture at all. If your foyer falls into the last category, skip this section entirely. If you do have a piece or two gracing your entryway, here's a general system for keeping it clean.

If all of that organizing has gotten you a bit out of breath, take a break—I think it's almost time for kick-off. Plop yourself in front of the tube with a bowl of munchies and a cold one. You can get back to the hall at half-time.

The Lazy Way

Tidy Tables and Chaste Chairs

That hall or entranceway table is really attractive, especially since it's no longer covered with everything but the kitchen sink. But it will still collect dust. Here's an easy way to keep it polished. You'll need (depending on the make-up of the furniture):

- Feather duster
- Furniture polish for wood furniture
- Soft cloth

Or

- Window cleaner for laminates, glass and mirrored pieces
- Paper towels

1. Depending upon the make-up of the table, dust it off with your feather duster, use a little furniture polish on a soft cloth, or spray it with window cleaner to make it shine.

2. Arrange a few family pictures and the plant that you got as a gift for Boss's Day.

3. Most important, keep it simple; the less you add to the tabletop, the less dust collects, and the less time it takes to clean.

Quick Floor Fixes

If you live in a fifth floor apartment and you have to take an elevator and walk down a long hall before reaching your front door, chances are you've already wiped off the

IF YOU'RE SO
INCLINED

You might want to add a table lamp for a nice, warm, evening glow. If you plug it into a timer, it will greet you on those dark winter's evenings when you trudge in late from work.

mud from your shoes before you've rung the doorbell. But if the outside is right on the other side of your front door, your entranceway will pick up all the wonders of nature. Your floor might be wood, carpet, tile, slate, or stone. But dirt is dirt, and someone's got to clean it.

Step by Step to Footprintless Floors

Here's an easy way to keep your floor shined. Unless you're living in an area where there is construction going on or at the foot of a volcano, you may want to vacuum twice a week at most and wash the floor once a week at best. Remember, if it's not dirty, don't clean it. You'll need (depending on the make-up of the flooring):

- Water
- Gentle floor cleaner like Spic and Span or Murphy's Oil Soap
- Mop

Or

- Wood cleaner
- Soft cloth or soft mop

Or

- Vacuum cleaner
- Electric broom

IF YOU'RE SO INCLINED

For many years, I have been using a product called Life O' Wood. It's a nice easy liquid to work with. It cleans and renews the wood and prevents it from drying out from the heat and air conditioning and leaves a nice shine. I pour some onto a soft cloth to clean wood floors (you could always use a rag on a sponge mop) and furniture. I also realized that you can use it on vinyl tile and varnished wood. Just add $1/2$ cup to one quart of warm water.

Place a rug that can be vacuumed in the front entrance during winter and then change to a mat that you can throw into the washing machine during warmer months.

1 Remove the top dust from all floors by vacuuming either with a vacuum cleaner or an electric broom. (If your floor is covered with carpeting, you're finished!)

2 Remove any area rugs or mats.

3 Dissolve a gentle floor cleaner in water. Follow the directions on the bottle or box for the proper proportions. Most of these cleaners can be used on everything from slate to hardwood.

4 Mop the floor. Rinse and squeeze the mop head several times during the project to keep it clean. Don't drown the floor; simply damp mop it.

5 Let the floor dry. This shouldn't take more than five minutes.

6 Replace the area rugs and doormat.

If you follow some of these tips, you will cut down on your cleaning. You can save not only time, but also energy. Because I know you'd rather do something else other than clean. (Let's face it—you bought this book!)

Under Cover

Don't let the outdoor elements ruin your hall floor. Place an outdoor mat outside your front door. They are made of a rough fabric which helps to scrape debris off your shoes.

You can also place an attractive washable doormat that sits right inside your front door. They are great for absorbing not only dirt but rain and snow, so that the elements don't get tracked into other rooms. These mats also are a great resting place for wet shoes. A simple doormat will save you repeated cleanups and unnecessary headaches and aggravation. Do yourself a favor. Try it; you'll like it.

- Place a doormat on the front porch that lets you wipe off your feet before you walk into the house. A few brisk shuffles at the front door will remove leaves, dirt, and mud from your shoes.
- If you live in a snowy climate, the outdoor mat won't cut it during the winter months. Inside the front door, put one that is decorative and can stand up to the elements.

Let's see. You've taken care of almost everything on the list. Just stash away those few things left and your future cleaning will be a breeze.

It's All in the Training

It's impossible to provide an easy access receptacle for all the belongings that family members leave around. Make sure that everyone in the household is clued in on the organizing system. Why not earmark one room at a time and take everyone on a tour? Make a family pact that everyone will try to pitch in to keep things as organized and tidy as they are.

After your entranceway is organized, and everyone's agreed to help keep it that way, celebrate your success with a movie, a special cake, a trip to the ice cream shop, or something else that your family likes to do together.

The Lazy Way

Getting Time on Your Side

	The Old Way	The Lazy Way
Finding the leather jacket you wore yesterday	10 minutes	30 seconds
Walking out of the house with mis-matched gloves	4 times	0 times
Tripping on the piles of stuff as you go up the stairs	Once a week	Never (there are no piles!)
Dusting the hall table	25 minutes	5 minutes
Cleaning the floor	15 minutes	8 minutes
Sorting the mail	7 minutes	3 minutes

Labor-Less Living Spaces

How much living do we really do in the living room? "Out of the living room!" "Don't play in the living room!" "The living room is for company." Living room? What a misnomer! Would a rose by any other name smell as sweet? Yes! That's why we have "the family room." The family room is the household space that gives permission to the family to recreate, snack, and wear comfortable clothing. (I'll bet that you're more formally dressed when the family gathers in the living room, aren't you?) And, finally, a desire to go back to basics has given us the "great room."

To summarize: every home contains a living space that may be labeled as the:

- Living room
- Family room

or the

- Great room

We're going to cover all these under living spaces, taking into consideration that some are more lived in than others.

EASY LIVING ROOM

There was a time when I would buy a new outfit, save it for something special, and have it hang in the closet, waiting to be worn. How, you ask, does this have anything to do with cleaning your living room? Well, I don't know about you, but I spent a great deal of time, effort, and money decorating my living room, only to have it sit empty most of the time. It's really a shame, because when we do use it, we enjoy friends and family, good food, mood-setting music, and a cocktail or two. Unfortunately, dust collects whether you use a room often or not.

Declutter Your Collectibles

My guess is that if your living room tends to look dirty, even though you don't use it that often, it is because of the clutter. We seem to use our living rooms to display items that we have collected over time. Your home is a reflection of you, your hobbies and tastes. It's fun to have assemblages of various types on display.

Unfortunately, the more treasures we have exhibited on tabletops, bookshelves, and pianos, the more work we make for ourselves. These pieces all need to be dusted and polished. A feather duster, or the like, will do the job on the items themselves, but, drats, you're going to have to pick up each ceramic frog, each antique purse, each beer stein to dust underneath it. Otherwise, the outline of your collectible will be delineated on the table when someone picks it up to admire it.

YOU'LL THANK YOURSELF LATER

Consider displaying your collectibles in clear boxes or picture frames. You'll cut down on the amount of dusting that you have to do if they are enclosed.

Once you've neatly stored some knickknacks out of sight, your cleaning time will be reduced to the time it takes to watch your favorite TV show, excluding the commercials. So let's get this show on the road. It's almost time for *Frasier.*

You have to organize the clutter and keep it under wraps. There are so many types of closed display cases that would look great as part of your décor and that would exhibit your items to their fullest beauty. Just picture your ceramic frogs on display in:

- An enclosed, shelved Lucite box that hangs on the wall
- A closed cabinet with lighted glass shelves
- A table that is constructed like a box with legs, complete with a hinged cover and glass top
- A china cabinet
- Picture frames (for smaller and flatter objects)

Admire your treasures and smile, because you are on your way out to play 18 holes.

Periodicals Are a Pushover

Maybe you don't collect magazines, but I'll bet you have some in your living room. Journals add character; journals speak of your interests and your intellect. It may be *National Geographic, Rolling Stone,* or *AARP.* A few magazines look great adorning the coffee table, but if you stack them too high you can't see the person sitting across from you. If you leave magazines scattered all over the place they look messy.

QUICK ⓝ PAINLESS

Don't feel as if you have to keep all of your collectibles in full view. Enjoy a few pieces at a time, store the rest, and rotate them when the mood strikes you. You'll never tire of that ceramic pig collection you great-aunt passed down to you!

Green plants add a lot to a room's décor. Caring for them, however, is another household chore. I find that smaller plants that can be walked (or larger plants that can be wheeled on a cart) to the sink for a good squirt at the faucet are the easiest to care for. Wet them down and let them drip dry in the sink.

Use your magazines to your cleaning advantage. Put just a few on top of the coffee table, and some underneath a sofa table, either in a basket or decorative box. Or just stack them, spines facing out, on the floor. The trick is simply to keep them together. Or try this unique suggestion: buy a magazine rack and house it next to your favorite chair.

No-Bother Bookcases

I love books and bookcases. I think they add a tremendous amount of color and character to a room. And, depending upon the titles, they can be quite impressive. (Unless, of course, you shop at Books-by-the-Yard.) I used to try to mix books with knickknacks, art prints, and photographs thinking that the combination added charm to my room. What they really added was mishmash to the mix. The bookcases looked messy, the room looked cluttered, and it was much more difficult to keep everything clean, with the dust bunnies rampantly multiplying.

A swift solution to skimming time off this cleaning chore is to fill the bookshelves mostly with books, with a decorative touch here and there. If you learn to use your feather duster with dispatch and style, it will take only a few fine flicks to sweep those cottontails into oblivion. (And if you don't read very often, and don't move the titles around too much, you'll rarely have to remove the books from the shelves to do a thorough book buffing.)

Tidy Tabletop Tips

Just as you put your collectibles under wraps, let's make a similar move with the conglomeration on the side table, the coffee table, and the sofa table. (I know that this sounds like a long and difficult project, but it's really not. Watch TV, listen to music, talk on the phone. You know, Double Duty it. You might even peruse a magazine or two before tossing them into the recycle bin. Enjoy this part of the project and look forward to easy sailing in the future.) Strip them bare and start from scratch. Begin with the coffee table. We already have a small pile of magazines perched prettily within arm's reach. Now lets add a pair of candlesticks, with candles, a lovely glass bowl filled with lemons, and a philodendron in a cachepot.

Set the coasters, small figurines, and other doodads aside. We'll take care of them in a minute.

Now, let's address the sofa table. This is probably where you have a lamp, a photograph, and a vase with flowers or some other nice green wash-and-wear plant.

Chances are there are a lot of other things on that table that belong somewhere else. So before you make the table look pretty, you have to clear it off. Remember that game "Pick out what doesn't belong?"

1 Put the gloves and scarves in the front hall closet or inside the seat of the Victorian hall chair.

2 Your briefcase goes in the picnic-like basket at the foot of the stairs to await the next trip to the second floor.

QUICK ⬭ PAINLESS

The drawer in the table might be the perfect spot for your car keys. If you do put them there, make sure they're in their own small container. (You don't want them to get misplaced once the drawer starts filling up.)

A drawer of a side table in the living room or a drawer in a chest of drawers in the hall may be the perfect location to store mail and the supplies you need for paying your monthly bills. This may not be the most comfortable spot, however, to sit when you are actually writing checks. Consider purchasing an organizer that can fit into the drawer but is portable enough to be moved to the area where you are going to work.

3 Set aside your keys as well as your Tic-Tacs and credit card slips. We'll get to those in a minute.

4 Last but not least, briskly strip the side table of hodge-podge. (Before you move on to step 5, since the table is clear, this is a good time to dust it. Check out "Tabletops Are Not for Toes.")

5 If you have a reading lamp for this space, put it in place.

6 Grab one of the covered baskets that you just bought to help you organize, and put your extra reading glasses into it.

7 Top off the table top with a book.

Of all the tables in your living room, this is the one that most likely has drawers. Perfect! We can now hide all that stuff that you put aside when you straightened up.

Depending upon where you open your mail, this table may be where you want to organize you bills, credit card slips, envelopes, stamps, everything that you need to pay your monthly bills. Fill one drawer with several small boxes that fit together like a puzzle and fill in the space. Allocate each of the following "pay the bill" items to a box:

- Bills: I have a little system I use so I won't forget to pay a bill. The minute that I open the statement, I write the date that the bill needs to be paid on the envelope in which the bill was sent. I drop the envelopes into a little basket, just large enough to hold them, in order of their due date.

- Envelopes, in case one is not included with the invoice.
- Postage stamps
- Pens
- Credit card slips (so that you can compare them with the credit card bill)
- Small calculator

Ideally, when finding a place for everything, and putting everything in its place, we should try to store supplies as close as possible to the area where we're going to use them. But sometimes a house or an apartment just doesn't lend itself to this perfect scheme. Then you have to create the adaptability.

Fluff and the Family Gallery

I never know what to do about family photos. I love to have them on exhibit in various locales around the house. They are my memories, my history, and the final proof of successful orthodontia. I love the challenge of finding the perfect frame to complement a particular photo, a frame that works as a whole with the dozens of other frames that embellish the snapshots adorning the room. But it is the ultimate family photo gallery challenge that drives me bonkers: keeping the dust under control. When you find yourself inscribing the names of those in the photograph in the dust on the frame's glass, you know you have a problem. One of my favorite cleaning tools, the feather duster, is the quickest solution.

IF YOU'RE SO
INCLINED

Buy photo albums similar to each other in style, fabric, and color. Put the album with the most recent snapshots on the coffee table. Line the others up on a bookshelf. Label the binding in gold leaf with your family monogram or crest and the period during which the pictures were taken. Then you'll always be able to lay your hands on that one particular picture that you're looking for.

But if your frames are intricately detailed, it takes more than a swish to solve the dust deluge. Here are a few no brainers that will keep your family shots more visible, give your salon more organization, and save you a lot of dusting effort.

- Frame the photos in similar frames (all wood, all metal, all black, or all painted) and hang them as if in a gallery on a large wall space. If you tire of a picture, or get an updated version, remove the photo from the frame and replace it with the newer model.

- Display a few of your most treasured pictures, with emphasis on few. I know it's hard to choose only a few, so why not consider setting some frames aside to hold a rotating gallery of snapshots. It will be fun to update the progress of your family's growth, and visitors will always have something new to look at.

- Keep unframed pictures, the ones that are waiting to be put into an album when you get the time, into containers for this specific purpose. Or use an old hat box or something else that goes well with your décor. Try not to display snapshots unframed. If someone sends you a great picture that they took of the two of you at the barbecue last summer (one you look at and say, wow, I really look terrific!), don't stick it into the corner of a frame that already has a picture in it or in a mirror frame—it will simply collect dust (and you may not be able to see that fabulous figure as well!).

IT'S EASY BEING CLEAN

Congratulations! Once again, you have conquered clutter. You're really getting the hang of it now. Don't bother blocking out a lot of time for tidying up the living room. You won't need it. Look around. What's there to do? Everything looks so neat. Let's zip through this cleaning project quickly and effortlessly. Don't even bother to call in the troops. This is small stuff; you won't need them.

Expressly Mobilize Those Supplies

There will be some rooms in your home that just won't lend themselves to hiding cleaning supplies. The living room is probably one of them. These supplies are most likely consigned to the kitchen or the pantry. If you've been clever enough to store living room cleaning supplies together, grabbing them will be hassle-free.

In Chapters 1 and 5 we talked about the different products that you'll use depending upon the make-up of your furniture. If you do not have any wood pieces, then, of course, you can forget about grabbing the furniture polish. Here's a quick checklist to facilitate faster pick-up. The optional items are listed at the end:

- Paper towels
- Rags (soft cloths)
- Window cleaner
- Feather duster
- Vacuum Cleaner and attachments

QUICK **П** *PAINLESS*

Still saving those single socks in hope of finding their mates? Put the loners to better use. Use them as dust cloths. You just put your hand inside as if it were a puppet, and dust away!

QUICK 🔘 PAINLESS

Optional

- Electric broom
- Furniture polish
- Carpet stain remover

Feather Duster Flexibility

Try these steps for easy cleaning:

- Clean from top to bottom.
- Work either clockwise or counter clockwise around the room.
- Save the sweeping or vacuuming for last.

1. Clean from top to bottom: Everything I've read by cleaning gurus says that you should clean from top to bottom. It makes sense. As you work, the dust and lint fall to the floor. Then the last thing that you do before calling it quits is vacuum, sweep, or dust. (You can jimmy rig your duster to a broom handle for a longer reach, or simply attach a rag to the bristles of the broom to catch the high cob webs. I own a product called a Static Duster that has a handle that telescopes for longer distance.)

2. I also like to work my way around the room. For instance, a petite grand piano stands in one corner of my living room. If I start in this corner, I dust the piano. (If there are a lot of fingerprints on the

wood, I might put a little Life O' Wood on a soft rag and wipe the areas of the piano that show the most prints.) I shortcut the rest of the piano dusting with a swift flick of the feather duster.

I've long since eliminated the family picture gallery from atop the piano. (Been there, done that. I'm into hassle-free housecleaning and this was a pain in the neck to move, dust, and replace.) The piano hood is always open; so, yes, some dust does accumulate on the hammers and strings. But I just take my feather duster and arpeggio my way right over the 88.

3. Moving right along, hip-hop over to the paintings behind the piano, and, with that wrist motion that you are beginning to perfect, flick off any little dust particles that have collected. If you're just dusting, all artwork can be handled the same way. But if you need to touch up a spot here and there, be careful.

If you have any questions about how to clean your framed pieces, you might ask someone at the store where you purchased them. If it's something that you found at a yard sale, or a piece that has been in your family for generations, you may want to take it to an antique shop for professional advice. Also try calling the curator's office or the education department of your local community art gallery for tips and ideas on the proper cleaning and storing of your works of art.

A COMPLETE WASTE OF TIME

The Three Worst Things to Do with Window Cleaner and Framed Artwork:

1. Spray onto a painted frame—the paint from the frame can end up on your cloth.

2. Squirt wood frames with a lot of liquid—they won't stay beautiful for long.

3. Overdo it. The pictures are not hermetically sealed in their frames—you don't want any liquid to seep in and ruin them.

Fluff Up the Furniture

Most of the time, all you have to do to straighten up your sofa and chairs is:

1. Plump up the cushions and the throw pillows.

2. Once a month or so, flip the cushions. Sunlight and air will tend to fade the upholstery, no matter how much you paid for it.

3. While you're flipping, take a peek to see if there are any crumbs, dust, (yuck!) dead bugs, or (yippee!) quarters in the crevices. (If your living room is hardly lived in, you may want to check for debris just a few times a year. The days following Christmas, Chanukah, the Fourth of July, and Thanksgiving would be appropriate.) One of the neat little attachments on your vacuum cleaner will suck up the remnants.

And, oh, look at that! While you were flipping the sofa cushions you discovered a grease stain. (You had a feeling your son was hiding something when he dashed out of the family room, piece of pizza in hand.) The best solution to the grease problem would have been to be able to counter attack it when it attacked the sofa. But we can't dwell on the past. If you do catch a stain fresh, follow the steps below:

1. Luckily, there are several brands of upholstery cleaner that can do the job. Be sure to read the instructions on the can. (I have been known not to, and inevitably did something wrong.)

YOU'LL THANK YOURSELF LATER

Order Scotch Garded fabric when you buy your next couch and have a fighting chance. (See Chapter 5.) You'll rarely have to encounter: "Oh, look, someone already turned this cushion. Might it have been to hide this grease stain? And who knows how long it has been sitting here? Will it ever come out?"

2. When you clean up a fresh stain, try blotting it first with a clean, white dry cloth or a paper towel, then put on the cleaning foam or fluid.

3. With a clean cloth, clean the spot from its border into the center. If you rub from the inside to the circumference, you may spread the stain even further.

We're on a roll now. The time has flown; we've only Mashed Potatoed through the first four songs on the CD. Let's finish the sofa. Put the cushions back and arrange the throw pillows. You know, a throw pillow is not just another a pretty face; it can be quite utilitarian. Throw pillows can:

- Disguise stains, rips and tears, and other slight imperfections.

- Give older pieces of furniture new life.

- Add color and decorative touches.

- Be used behind the backs of people of a more petite stature to help them sit up straighter and allow them to get their feet on the ground. (Being a bit over five feet myself, I truly appreciate this point.)

Tabletops Are Not for Toes

One, two, cha cha cha. Three, four, dust some more. Now you've got the rhythm, this is a breeze. The organization that we went through at the beginning of the chapter really paid off. If you can keep your belongings under wraps, hidden in closed containers, and free from the extra doodads that bring out the dust bunnies, you will

QUICK ⬭ PAINLESS

Does that stain look like melted butter from your recent lobster fest? A great grease remover is talc. (Talc is not baby powder; it is an ingredient in baby powder. Do not use baby powder to remove oily stains; it has oil in it to keep the baby's tushie soft and will defeat the whole purpose.) Sprinkle some on the stain and let it absorb the blotch. Then vacuum up the residue. The stain is gone!

cut the clutter and the pick-up time in half. (And you'll be a dream of a dancer to boot.)

There are two tables to tackle before we bring out the vacuum cleaner. The one near the easy chair looks pretty good.

1. Just put your glasses into the little basket or holder that you bought to keep them in sight.

2. Someone left a glass sitting right on top of the wood. (There were coasters on the coffee table to use for this very purpose, too.) Oh, dear. The ice in the glass melted, the glass sweated, and dripped water onto the table, leaving a perfectly formed ring. There's a great little trick for removing water stains from a wood table. Rub petroleum jelly into the wood, and the stain disappears.

The last piece of furniture in the room is the table behind the sofa. It may hold a lamp, a pretty porcelain covered dish, and perhaps a piece of art.

1. The lamp receives a few flicks of the feather duster.

2. The porcelain dish rinses off with a squirt of window cleaner and dries off with a paper towel. The material of your work of art, or other object on the table, will dictate what type of cleaner you use—whether it gets a quick shower or a quick tickle. If your table happens to be Formica, then it doesn't matter if the table receives a few drips of window cleaner, since that's what you'll use to clean it.

3. If your table is wood, I recommend that you remove the object and give it a spritz of window cleaner

elsewhere. Then either dust off the table or give it a quick polish with your spray wood cleaner and soft cloth.

Vacuuming Really Sucks

Do you know why vacuuming is the best? Because it's last! It means that we're almost finished! (I think that the Conga can get our blood moving through this last step. And it will also keep us moving in a straight line.)

In Chapter 2 you may have read about all of the different types of power tools available. If so, choose your weapon and let's get going.

I suggest that you:

1. Start in the back corner of the room and work your way to the exit. It's kind of like the concept of not painting yourself into a corner. If you have plush carpeting that shows footprints, and would like to see the carpet as smooth as silk for at least a minute and a half, this is a good route to take.

2. Every few weeks or so, at the same time that you're vacuuming the carpet, you can also hit those high points of housecleaning that we Lazyites do not need to do on a weekly basis. (Remember, if it ain't broke, don't fix it; if it ain't dirty, don't clean it.)

3. Use one of the vacuum attachments to go over the drapes, shutters, or blinds.

4. Pick the skinny, angled attachment to get into the corners of the room.

QUICK n PAINLESS

To remove wax candle drippings from table cloths and placemats, cover the wax with a brown paper lunch bag or a piece of a brown paper grocery bag and gently apply a warm iron until the wax lifts from the cloth and adheres to the bag.

So that you don't have to wash your dust mop each time you use a liquid cleaner such as Life O' Wood, wrap a clean rag around the mop and fasten it to the handle with a twist tie or rubber band. When you finish your floors, remove the rag and throw it out or into the washing machine.

5. The brush works well on the moldings as well as baseboards. No need to get carried away, though. No one is going to stare at the ceiling. Just be sure that you knock out the cobwebs.

If your living room floor is hardwood covered with an area rug, you have a few choices on how to handle the wood that shows:

- Use a soft dust mop.
- Use an electric broom.
- Use a vacuum cleaner that has the ability to go from carpet to floor.
- Use a dust buster. You'll have to bend over (oooooh my aching back!).
- Use a mop dipped into 1 tablespoon Murphy's Oil Soap that has been dissolved in a quart of water.
- Use ½ cup Life O' Wood dissolved in warm water.

I sometimes find that when I vacuum my area rugs, I turn into Daffy Duck. The center of the rug never seems to cause a problem; it's the fringe on each end of the carpet that I get into a scuffle with. It doesn't matter how careful I am, how slowly I try to sneak up on it, I continually get the fringe sucked up into the vacuum cleaner. I then become all crazed and jerky trying to find the off switch or pulling out the plug. My solution to this problem is to either disregard the fringe, or buy a new vacuum that has a suction regulator (see Chapter 2).

I, personally, am not in the market at this time for a new piece of equipment. So I've decided, what difference does it make? I don't think that the fringe gets that dirty to worry about it. You can always shake it out. Doesn't this sound less frustrating than pulling it out of the vacuum? If it becomes an annoyance, lean over and comb it with your fingers.

Quick Tips for the Floors:

1 Vacuum all carpets.

2 Move the area rugs and doormats to clean underneath them.

3 Wash the floors with a product suited for the flooring material.

4 Let the floor dry.

5 Replace throw rugs and door mats.

You most likely will want to move a small chair, a plant, or a stack of magazines when you vacuum. If you feel that you need to do a major cleaning, or you know (or can smell) that something is aging under the sofa, be sure that you don't move the furniture by yourself. Simple under-the-chair jobs are easily accomplished with the vacuum cleaner hose and all those other handy-dandy attachments.

YOU'LL THANK YOURSELF LATER

When your Poodle makes a puddle, don't drown it in ammonia—that only intensifies the smell of urine to the pooch and attracts her back to the same spot. Ask your pet store for a compound that will neutralize the smell for both you and Fifi.

Okay. Close your eyes. Picture what your living room looked like 30 minutes ago. Open! Look at it now. Terrific! Keeping the living room neat is no longer a chore. Straightening up from now on will run you less than 20 minutes, because your organization is complete. The trick, of course, is to keep up this blueprint.

FRIVOLOUS, FLEXIBLE FAMILY ROOMS

Relax, change into your jeans, and take off your shoes. I called for the pizza (I hope you like anchovies and artichoke hearts); it will be delivered in about 35 minutes. That should give us more than enough time to put the family room in order. You've already got the formula. Now all you have to do is apply it.

This room is a bit more of a challenge than the living room, since this is the room that the kids, their friends, the dog, the two cats, and your spouse (and you, of course), live in. The equipment and paraphernalia that accompanies even the smallest tot these days is mind-boggling. Our grandson is only a few months old. Before he was born, our son's family room was decorated with a sofa, love seat, chair, TV, stereo and speakers, cocktail table, side tables, lamps, and plants. Now the view from the bridge includes a portable crib or bassinet, infant seats of two different varieties, an infant swing, small toys, and a play gym. I don't think that *Architectural Digest* is going to be by to shoot a layout anytime soon, but our son's family might get a call from *Parents* magazine.

I know that very few homes with small children have enough space to tuck away all the equipment that is needed in order to bring up the well-adjusted child. I know, from personal experience, that every parent goes to bed at night blessing the inventor of the infant swing. There is no way that I would suggest hiding that piece of equipment in a place that would make it difficult to reach. The resolution is to live with the best accouterments, and eliminate the rest.

Happily and Handily Hide It

If you are not in that phase of life where children and their *objets d'art* are the center of your world, you might go back to the living room section of this chapter and apply it to your family room. If your life after work revolves around family, children, and their playthings, you can certainly apply the basics of the living room section to the family room, but with a few twists and turns.

It's not just children who trash the family room. Many adults, professional and otherwise, clutter it with things they use for work and play. You, too, must deal with your toys, CDs, and computer disks. Sort them, stack them, hide them, and put them back where they belong when you're finished using them.

The messiness of a family room in a home with small children is probably mostly on the floor and furniture. If you have a toddler, sweep your tables clean of anything that's breakable, has sharp points, or tears easily. During the day, you may, of necessity, have to take your tables down to the basics, four legs and a top. Put all the

QUICK ⬤ PAINLESS

If you hide all of your precious belongings, like the glass elephant your uncle brought from India, for fear of an accident, you may end up not seeing them until 18 years after the birth of your youngest child. Instead, incorporate some of them into the scheme of the items that you keep on your mantle, or on the top shelf of the bookcase. If there's not enough room to exhibit everything at once, consider rotating your mementos from month to month.

IF YOU'RE SO
INCLINED

A benefit of purchasing standing furniture units is that they can be moved from the family room to a den, to a child's room, to the basement for extra storage, or with you to another home. That chest that's now full of toys and games could later hold an extra TV and VCR, or vice-versa.

objects you removed in a basket, and store them on a top shelf. After the tots are tucked in for the night, bring out your basket of toys and play with:

- The remote control
- The book you've been reading
- Your extra pair of reading glasses
- Your stash of chocolate-covered cherries

Remember how we dealt with some of the magazines and plants in the hall and living room? By stacking them under a few of the tables we made things neater and added some interesting decorative touches. If you have tots who might mangle or consume such stuff, consider using these spaces for toys, puzzles, and children's books. Hinged baskets can be great receptacles for these items. All they need is a little flip to open and close.

Another way to conquer clutter and organize the room is to have as many closed cabinets as possible. The family room must be a natural space for storage. I've noticed that lots of builders these days include built-ins in their blueprints. The shelves on the top may be open while those on the bottom are covered with doors. If your family room did not come with built-ins and remodeling is not within your current budget, you may wish to consider freestanding furniture units that are available to serve this purpose. They can be found in a large variety of styles, materials, and price ranges.

By hiding objects in either custom built or purchased furnishings, you remove all the little dust magnets from sight and make your room appear so much cleaner. Some of these spaces are designed to hide:

- TV
- VCR
- Stereo equipment
- CDs, tapes, and records (if you still own any)
- Games
- Family videos
- Unorganized photos
- Crayons and coloring books
- Jigsaw puzzles
- Unread newspapers
- Magazines you don't want cut up for school projects

Another shortcut to organizing the kids' cache is to tag the storage vessels. Print the contents on labels and affix them to the holders. If the kids are too young to read, draw pictures (a crayon, a piece of a puzzle) on the card. If they are really young, choose boxes of different colors or with different colored lids in which they can keep their belongings, e.g., purple is for puzzle, blue is for block, etc.

Review Your Reserves

Now that we've put all the clutter behind closed doors, we're ready to do a quick cleaning. Let's go over what you'll need:

- Paper towels
- Rags (soft cloths)

QUICK n' PAINLESS

Stash the crayons and coloring books in a heavy-duty plastic container with a lid (like those made by Tupperware or Rubbermaid). That way, the kids can see what's inside the box without tearing apart the whole cupboard, you can throw the container onto the top shelf of the dishwasher for cleaning and sanitizing, you won't have to search everywhere for tangerine and violet, and everybody needs a good Tupperware "burp" once in a while.

YOU'LL THANK YOURSELF LATER

Quarter your children's items on the lowest shelves in the room. It will make it so much easier for them to retrieve, and it will make you so much happier when they can put the particulars away.

- Window cleaner
- Feather duster
- Vacuum cleaner and attachments

Optional

- Electric broom
- Furniture polish
- Carpet stain remover

Let's Dance Through the Drudgery

If you follow the basic pattern for cleaning the living room, you can zip through the family room before you can say zippity-do-dah. The toughest and most time-consuming part of the job is behind you. Your room is organized and the clutter is gone; day- to-day objects are disguised from the world and, maybe more important, are hidden from public view and from much of the dust and grime.

Here are the steps; you pick the music. If the troops are joining in the fun, why not choose songs that they would know and enjoy? If you have a rechargeable electric broom (which doesn't need to be plugged in), get your seven year old to macarena with you. You can tell them that it is a real treat to be able to use this big person's appliance.

Let's check off the chores:

- Clear the clutter and store the stash.
- Flick your feather duster, have a real blast.

- Polish the wood, but don't overdo.
- Windex the glass, and Formica, too.
- Fluff the cushions and the throw pillows.
- And vacuum it up—see, isn't this mellow!

This has really been quite a task! You've put everything in order in almost no time flat. This was not just a project from which you'll see results for just a few short hours. You've done such a great job sorting and organizing that even when the kids come home from school and sprawl out on the sofa, things will not magically go back to the way they were. From now on, the living room will be easier to keep clean because there is less in plain sight to make dirty.

THE GREAT ROOM

I suggest that, if you have children, you treat your great room the same way you treat the family room. If you don't have kids living at home, follow the cleaning pattern for the living room. Either way, once you take the clutter out of sight, the rest is a breeze. If you clean as you go, your life will be much simpler, have less stress, and be a lot more fun.

You organized and cleaned at least one and possibly two rooms. You deserve a round of applause. This warrants some serious private time. Luxuriate in a hot bubble bath. Surround yourself with scented candles. And, hey, why not, you deserve it, pour yourself a glass of champagne!

The Lazy Way

Getting Time On Your Side

	The Old Way	The Lazy Way
Sprucing up the living room for company	60 minutes	20 minutes
Finding all the pieces for the jigsaw puzzle	15 minutes	2 minutes
Getting the troops to help pick up the family room	10 minutes	4 minutes
Looking for the remote control	3 minutes	1 minute
Dusting the bookcases	8 minutes	4 minutes
Watering the plants	10 minutes	4 minutes

Chop-Chop Kitchen Chores

The kitchen is, has been, and always will be the hub of our home. I thought that when the kids were grown and out of the house, we'd be out of the kitchen and into a restaurant. I thought that we executed enough homework projects at the kitchen table to last anyone a lifetime of precious memories. I figured that we'd at least be spending our evenings sitting in the family room curled up by a crackling fire. I'm not going to tell you that none of the above has come true, but we still spend a great deal of time in our kitchen.

We've discovered that it doesn't matter whether there are two or ten members of the family living at home—the kitchen gets very dirty very easily. Cooking, eating, grabbing a snack, all cause spills, crumbs, and dirty dishes. When you're in a hurry, you leave cupboard doors open, dishes on the counter, and last night's newspaper on the table. I thought that when we were only two mature adults at home, there would not be any tracked in dirt, book bags, and coats dropped on the back of kitchen chairs anymore. I was wrong. The book bags are now briefcases and laptop computers, and the distance between the kitchen chair and the front hall closet has not gotten any shorter.

In fact, we seem to spend more time in the kitchen. It's convenient; it's comfortable; it's easy. The kitchen is where we unwind, watch the news, talk long distance to the kids, and eat. And, no matter how you cut it, eating is messy, even if it's take-out. Then there are the nights that my husband and I take pleasure in cooking together. We seem to use every pot and pan in the cupboard, manage to spill something onto the floor, and make a mess out of the microwave.

We've added a few accouterments to this room since those early days of tater tots and finger paintings. A small TV holds a prominent position in the corner near the kitchen table. (Watching TV was a big no-no in the days when our table was crowded with kids, in the days before college and eating on the run. Dinner was the time that the family shared school stories, not reruns of "Gilligan's Island.") Over the years, we've also made a lot of changes to our kitchen's general décor. We've added the microwave, an icemaker, a convenient center island, three-zone adjustable lighting, and a generally more attractive atmosphere in which to work. Why move to a different room? We've got it all in this one.

This room is meant to be the center of your family's world. Some things never change; they just acquire more conveniences. In fact, in some cases, you wonder why family rooms, living rooms, and dining rooms are needed at all. For most of us, our lives have become less formal.

And our lives have become more hectic. Our lives need a place to unwind. The kitchen is the answer. And yet the kitchen can be one of the dirtiest rooms in the house.

As in every chapter, here I provide you with tips on how to get rid of and organize the clutter in your kitchen before you start cleaning. It's not the spaghetti sauce stain on the counter top or the rice crusted on the stove top that you notice when you walk in. It's the dirty dishes piled in the sink, the dry cleaning hanging over the chair, and a week's worth of mail piled on top of the counter.

(For those of you who live in a home with a very small kitchen, you might want to flip past the next several pages and go right to the heart of the matter: sink, stove, refrigerator, and floor. In some cases, you might not even want to look at the section on counter space if you're working with a two-by-four.)

ORGANIZATION: A FORKFUL OF FORM, FUNCTION, AND FLEXIBILITY

It's all in the way you organize it. In previous chapters, we've strolled through some systematizing tips that you can use to eliminate visible clutter. We're going to apply some of them to help you conquer your kitchen chaos:

- Put it away and out of sight.
- Stash it in a closed repository.
- Stow it where it takes the least number of steps to retrieve it.
- After you use it, put it back in the same place.

QUICK ⟨II⟩ PAINLESS

Instead of rustling through your kitchen drawers to find a wooden spoon, keep your most often used utensils right on top of the stove. Stand them up in a pretty pitcher, canister, or tall glass container. Just make sure that the receptacle is easy to clean.

In order to get the full capacity from your dishwasher, find the handbook that came with the machine and read the directions on how to load your dishwasher.

Doing the Dishes Is a Lot of Crock

Let's face it: Dirty dishes make a kitchen appear messy. If there are three people in your family and each one leaves his or her dish on the table, on the counter, or in the sink, it will seem as though everywhere you look, there are dirty dishes.

However, if, after you dine, all three of you remove your dishes from the table and place them into the sink, you have made a short step toward total uncluttering. But do not pass Go and do not collect $200. You have simply concentrated the mishmash into the sink. You can still see the dishes.

Loading and Unloading Zone

If each of you saunters over to the dishwasher with your dirty dishes and deposits them into it, then in no time flat, and with very little effort, some of the kitchen clutter will vanish before your very eyes. (For in fact, a dishwasher is a closed container in which your soiled pottery is hidden from public scrutiny.)

One of the first steps toward conquering clutter and getting yourself on the road to spotlessness is to eliminate some of the steps that it now takes to put all the rubble away. Perhaps you've resorted to piling clean dishes on the counter since it's really a chore, in every sense of the word, to unload the dishwasher because you find yourself trekking back and forth from one end of the kitchen to the other, burdened with awkward armloads of dishes. I offer you three choices on how to resolve this annoyance:

Unloading the Dishwasher

I provide you with three options:

A. Ridiculously Radical Rotations

1 Place the dirty dishes on one side of the dishwasher racks and the clean dishes on the other.

2 Eat from the clean side, and deposit on the dirty side.

3 When there is nothing on the clean dish side, and the opposing side is full, it's time to run the dishwasher! (Use those cute little magnets on the outside of the door that say "clean" and "dirty" to remind you which side you're to eat from during this rotation.)

B. Are They Stacked!

1 Unload the full dishwasher onto a nearby counter.

2 Divide and stack the items into groups determined by which cupboard they belong in (dishes, platters, glasses, etc.).

3 Place each stack in its proper cupboard. You have minimized the number of steps that you have to take in order to finish the task.

QUICK ⟨n'⟩ PAINLESS

Silverware holders are usually portable. Lift out the entire utensil basket, carry it to your flatware drawer, and discharge its contents.

In 1964, I purchased a plastic covered wire dish organizer for my cupboard. It permits me to store eight five-piece place settings of my china on one double width cupboard shelf. What a great organizer! And they are still available, today.

C. Keep 'Em Close at Hand

1 Empty the kitchen cupboards and drawers that are closest to the dishwasher. This may mean either rearranging your staples or tossing out stuff that's useless or past the point of consumption.

2 Place your china, flatware, and pots and pans in the cupboards closest to the dishwasher.

Dishpan Hands

If your home or apartment is sans dishwasher, it doesn't mean that you have to spends loads (no pun intended) of time washing dishes. Here are a few quick tips to speed up the job:

1. When you're cooking, fill the sink with warm soapy water. As you finish with a pot or dish, put it into the sink to soak. If you have a double sink, rinse the dishes off on one side and then soak on the other.

2. Put all utensils into a pot or bowl filled with warm soapy water to prevent your blindly reaching into the sink and cutting yourself on a knife.

3. Wash the dishes with a sponge or dishrag. Use a steel soap pad to remove any caked on food.

4. Rinse the dishes in warm water.

5. Stand the clean dishes in a dish drain that has a tray to catch the drips as they dry.

6. Drip dry as many of the dishes as possible. You may want to dry crystal with a linen tea towel to prevent spots from forming.

7. When the dishes are dry, put everything into the cupboards and drawers where they belong.

Whether you have a dishwasher or wash your dishes by hand, there are two important things to remember to keep dish clutter to a minimum:

- Don't leave dirty dishes in the sink.
- Put clean dishes back into the cupboard.

Bravo! You met the mess straight on! Now you may collect the $200. Getting rid of dirty dishes is one of the easiest and least time consuming clean-up chores that anyone, of any age, can carry out.

A Ledged Countertop

People see messy before they see dirty. By putting dirty dishes directly into the dishwasher, you have taken one giant step toward a neat kitchen. Now let's tackle the countertops. We've already mentioned that the kitchen is the hub of the household. I'll bet that each of your family members comes home, marches into the kitchen, arms laden, and plops everything onto the counter. In case you haven't noticed, the piles on the countertops multiply in direct proportion to the number of persons who live under your roof. And the variety of items then becomes augmented ten-fold. Even if you are your home's only resident, your bundle probably contains a few of the following:

- Folders, loose papers, and a pamphlet from work
- A few groceries you grabbed at the corner store

YOU'LL THANK YOURSELF LATER

Prevent caked-on food from taking a slice out of your fun. If your dishwasher is older and crotchety like mine, a good rinse or a quick spray with a light solution of dishwashing detergent and water before you put your crusty vessels into the machine will save you from re-washing or, perish the thought, scrubbing them later.

- The shirts you picked up at the cleaners
- Today's newspaper
- The magazine you spotted at the newsstand, the one you've been waiting for all month
- The mail (haven't I seen this some place before?)
- Your keys (ditto)

Here are some choices for a final resting-place for your keys:

- In the hall in a basket.
- In the living room inside a box in the top drawer of the side table.
- On a decorative hook especially designed for your keys, which hangs on the wall in your kitchen

Good! The hook in the kitchen it is. Now let's move on to the mail.

I know, we've also talked about the mail before. But I don't know what your home is like. Do you live in an apartment where you pick up your mail from a box in the lobby or front hall? Do you reside in a house, and if you do, do you normally come in through the front door or the garage? Do you pick up your mail at a mailbox near the curb as you drive in, stop off at the front porch to grab it from the box, or does your front door have a mailslot? The key question after you answer these is what do you do with the mail after you walk into your home? And what tricks can you perform so that the mail does not become an eyesore in whatever room you

IF YOU'RE SO
INCLINED

Maybe the time has come for you to make a decision about where you're going to store the mail and keys. They've been in almost every room we've discussed!

choose to go through it? For many of us, we sort through the mail in the kitchen, and probably leave piles of it there, too. May I suggest that you:

- Sort your mail near a waste basket so that the junk mail never touches the countertop.

- Look at your bills right away (yuck) and throw out all the little inserts that are of no interest to you.

- Put the bills into the drawer/box/basket/container that you have assigned for this purpose.

- Read all of your correspondence and invitations. Throw out any envelopes, as well as the letters that need not be saved.

- Tack the invitations onto a bulletin board, or use a magnet to hold them on the refrigerator, or mark the information on your calendar, or slip them into your appointment book.

- Take the cellophane off the magazines and toss that into the trash. If more than one journal arrived today, be sure that it gets to the magazine rack, basket, or is stacked under the table that you've designated for this purpose. If the periodicals go upstairs, drop them into the picnic basket-like hamper at the foot of the stairs for the next person who ascends to carry up. (Many of these tips were discussed in Chapter 5, "Keep It Clean Without Becoming the Maid," Chapter 6, "Hallowed Halls in Half the Time," and Chapter 7, "Labor-Less Living Spaces.")

YOU'LL THANK YOURSELF LATER

If you don't know what to do with all your sets of keys, a great investment is a decorative holder that hangs on the wall. These pieces come in a wide variety of colors and designs that fit any décor. The keys are suspended on cup-like hooks. Some designs even have compartments for bills as well as a small bulletin board for important messages.

If the coat closet is just not "en route" when you enter the house, consider installing big coat hooks either next to the back door or near the kitchen. (If you're lucky enough to have a mud room, this is a great place to hang up the outerwear.) If you have little ones, install a few hooks at their height.

Coping with Coats

You're quickly relieving the counter of its clutter. Keep it up! But what happened to your jacket after you dumped your stuff in the kitchen? Oh, no. What's that on the kitchen chair? If you hang up your outerware in the closet as soon as you deposit your packages, the job will be done; your jacket won't be lying around adding mess.

Picture this: It's your magazine dream kitchen. As you walk into the room, there are big doors that, when opened, reveal individual compartments designed for each member of the family. In these stalls you hang your coat, quarter your briefcase, hang your keys, and put your science project for safe keeping. Everything you'll need as you leave the house in the morning is in one place. In my imagination, there's also a piping hot cup of cappuccino eagerly awaiting me in a cutting-edge spill-proof travel mug.

Dream on, McDuff. But you get the idea, don't you? Create a space in a convenient location where you can store the items you'll regularly need in the morning.

It Chops, It Slices, It Blends. No, Wait—It Cleans!

How many appliances do you have taking up your counter space, or lack there of? Do any, or all, of these ring a bell?

- Toaster
- Can opener
- Mixer

- Coffee maker
- Grinder for coffee beans
- Blender and food processor
- Microwave oven
- Portable convection oven

If you had these gadgets all operating at once, you'd trip a circuit breaker, for sure. It's no wonder you don't have any room to cook. Moreover, though you can't call apparatus clutter, there's enough of it to cover every inch of the counter. That means crumbs congregate in hidden corners, spills mysteriously disappear underneath equipment, and dust accumulates both on the appliances themselves, as well as in those now hard-to-reach areas of the countertop.

You have two choices:

1. Routinely clean all appliances and countertops, moving the equipment, of course, to scrub underneath.

2. Make some of these wonder toys disappear.
   (Personally, I prefer number 2.)

You can decide to play Houdini with either the smaller equipment, or the appliances you don't use that often. For example, the cupboard above the space where the coffee maker sits would be the perfect location for the coffee grinder. You may also want to place the coffee filters, mugs, and sugar or sugar substitute there.

The convection oven and the microwave are usually immovable objects. Now it's decision time: the toaster,

IF YOU'RE SO
INCLINED

When was the last time that you used your bread machine? Your pasta maker? Why not store your rarely used appliances in a cupboard underneath the counter, since they're just collecting grime, and save the precious space for equipment that you use every day.

Before you put the toaster away, turn it upside down and shake it over the sink. Then flip it right side up, open the trap doors on the bottom, and shake it again. This eliminates crumbs dropping to sneak out of the trap doors and land on the bottom of the storage area.

the food processor, or the mixer. At least one of these contraptions has to go underground. How often do you use the mix master and all the attachments that arrived with it? (Like a dough hook. Now there's a real dust collector in my house. I need a dough hook as badly as I need a meat hook, a fishhook, or a Captain Hook.) Relegate the mixer to a lower cupboard shelf until you need it. Choose a lower shelf. The machine is a bit heavy and awkward, and it's better to lift it up to the counter than to have it fall on your head when you're bringing it down.

Some people use their toaster daily, and their food processor rarely. The only time that I make toast is on the weekends, but even if I made it more often, I would choose to put this appliance down under because it's easier to move than the food processor with all it's attachments. Evaluate how often you use each of your appliances so that you can decide which ones you want to keep on top of the countertops and which ones can be moved below. Look! There's actually workspace on the counter. Good for you.

Condiments, Cupboards, and Cotchkes (Doodads, Knickknacks, and the like)

Everything is shaping up beautifully. The elbowroom on the counters is expanding as we speak. There are just a few more things to take care of before you move on. It will probably be more convenient to leave the knives in the wooden block on the counter near the cutting board, rather than put them into a drawer. You won't have to go rummaging around to find a paring knife, and you'll avoid nicked fingers, to boot.

The big salt and pepper shakers can stay—put them near the stove—but the spices should really go behind closed doors. You really do like to cook, don't you? Get a load of those spices! There must be dozens of them. If you keep them on top of the counter, they'll take up space and, especially if they're near the stove, become coated with grease, which then works as kind of a glue for dust and kitchen grime. And you don't want to have to wash off each and every individual little jar, do you? I didn't think so. So, let's:

1 Empty the small cupboard right near the stove. (Put the cans of soup and tuna fish in another cupboard on the other side of the kitchen.)

2 Prepare the cupboard so that it will handily hold the spice jars.

3 I recommend buying a Lazy Susan for each shelf. Arrange the spice jars around the circumference of the turntable.

Considering your cookbook collection, you must try quite a few recipes. Do you ever find yourself tripping over one of those books? There's a quick solution to the cookbook dilemma, if your kitchen is blessed with a small desk or a few shelves tucked away in a corner. Plop the books there, neatly and decoratively, of course.

Otherwise, here are a few suggestions on where to store your cache of cookbooks:

Congratulations! All you've moved is the coffee grinder, (a drip in the percolator of life), but, as they say in real estate, it's location, location, location. In one short, swift move you have saved yourself innumerable steps and made your mornings much easier. You've organized all the coffee brewing equipment in one area. Tomorrow, perk up a pot without even moving your feet from the floor.

The Lazy Way

If remodeling your kitchen is in your future, there is a feature that you may wish to consider called an appliance garage. You open the garage door, which looks like the top to a rolltop desk, use the appliance, roll the garage door back down, and the toaster is out of sight and out of splash, spill, and dust range.

- A shelf in your pantry.

- Add a free-standing bookcase to that empty wall in your kitchen.

- Add a shelf or two to an empty wall.

- On a cupboard shelf. In fact, remember the cupboard that you rearranged to store your spices? If there isn't anything assigned to the space that's left on the top, that's perfect. (Unless, like me, you're in the five-foot category. We'd better search for something closer to the floor.)

- The back of the deepest counter in the kitchen. Line up the books between the microwave and the wall.

Retrenching Your Chotchkes

My baby is 27, and I still have the Mother's Day gift that she made for me when she was in Brownies. It hasn't moved in all these years from where I installed it the day she gave it to me. It hangs on the lip of the hood over my stove. It's a wooden spoon, tied with a bow of green and yellow yarn; there are still a few dried flowers, holding on for dear life, that she carefully pasted onto the bowl of the wooden spoon. (I should have recognized her potential as a Martha-do-alike, even then.) I guess I'm just an old softie. I also have a small plaque sitting on my stove top that my son gave me, when he was 9, "To the world's greatest Mom." Pshaw! (So then, why doesn't he call?)

Everyone has personal chotchkes they need to surround themselves with, even in the kitchen. The trick is to keep these treasured possessions to a minimum, or behind glass doors, so that they don't interfere with neat and tidy, or become magnets for grease and grime. Your cleaning is supposed to be hassle-free, right?

The kitchen has a big advantage that no other room in the house does; it already comes with closed cupboards and drawers, and if you are fortunate, a pantry. There's lots of wonderful space to work with, right? Not always. Unless this really is your dream kitchen, there never seem to be enough cabinets and compartments to take care of all the items that you'd like to stow away, out of sight.

At the same time you're eliminating clutter from around the room, you're going to have to straighten out some of the same cupboards and drawers to make room for the things that were cluttering the kitchen.

Cleaning Out the Cupboards

This is a cinch: You'll need:

- Trashcan
- Picnic hamper

1 Throw out what's garbage.

2 Pull out whatever belongs in another room.

3 Tuck it into the hamper for the trip.

YOU'LL THANK YOURSELF LATER

Your stove is one of the greasiest places in your kitchen. The fewer items you keep near the burners, the fewer items you have to degrease.

To eliminate searching through your cupboard to find the right lid for that pot, store it on the pot it belongs to. If you are limited to space and need to stack pots in pots, use shelf dividers and keep the lids, standing up on their sides on a shelf, right over the pots they go with.

4 Wipe out the gunk that's been accumulating all this time in the bottom of the drawer.

5 Fill up the niche, again, with the new stash. Try to put your new items as close as possible to the appliance or area it's going to serve.

Kitchen designers will tell you that you should not have to take many steps while working in your kitchen. Everything should be practically at your fingertips. A well-organized kitchen will facilitate an almost effortless existence.

Store:

- Dishes, silverware, and glasses near the dishwasher.
- Pots, pans, and casseroles near the stove.

Keep:

- Knives near the cutting board.
- Spices and herbs near the preparation counter or the stove.
- Baking pans near the oven.
- Dish towels and aprons near the sink.
- Storage containers, aluminum foil, plastic wrap, and plastic storage bags near the preparation area.

GETTING DOWN AND DIRTY

Remember how, at the beginning of this chapter, we chatted about all the hearth, home, and fuzzy stuff that goes with thoughts of the kitchen? How the kitchen is the hub of the home, the place where everyone gathers, a room for entertaining, a home office, a homework haven, project central, and oh, yes, a room in which we prepare meals and eat them.

Please keep all of this in mind as you clean up, because unless you perform this task right before you leave the house, padlock the doors, and are the first one home at night, I guarantee that the kitchen will always have a little "lived in" look. The picture in the *This House is Gorgeous* magazine of a sparkling countertop decorously accented with a bud vase holding one perfect rose sitting next to a freshly baked crumbless loaf of bread does not exist outside of Oz.

Don't Forget the Supplies

All the cleaning supplies that you need for this job are right in this room. You may want to look back at Chapter 1 for a quick reminder. Take them out of the cupboard and set them in a convenient spot. If you have a center island, it would be ideal. You can reach whatever you need from any spot in the kitchen.

You should have:

- Scouring pads with self-contained soap
- Sponges
- Rubber gloves
- Paper towels
- Window cleaner
- Floor cleaning product for your type of floor
- Bleaching cleanser
- Pine scented cleaner

YOU'LL THANK YOURSELF LATER

If you break a glass, sweep up the broken pieces, being careful not to cut yourself. Then wet a good thickness of paper toweling and slowly go over the spot where the glass broke. Any remnants of glass will cling to the wet paper. Glass really scatters when it breaks. Wipe the towel in extra-wide movements to guarantee that those shards don't become shrapnel.

- Mildew cleaner, if you have tile on the backsplash
- White vinegar

If you have to go into another room to get the vacuum, electric broom, mop and bucket, or the mop vac, hurry up. I'm just itching to get started.

Humming Your Way to Harmony

The clutter is under control, out of sight and out of mind. The dishes are in the dishwasher. Don't bother with the CDs this time. You're going to go through this project so quickly that you'll only get to hear two tracks at best. Just hum. Let's attack this kitchen cleaning as a project that will leave the cookery with a nice, warm, lived-in feeling.

Kitchen Once-Over

You'll need:

- Duster with the extender arm
- Electric broom or vacuum cleaner
- Window cleaner
- Paper towels
- Sponge
- Detergent

1 Start at the top and work your way down. Use the extender arm on the feather or static duster to reach the high places first.

2 Start at one side of the room and work your way around.

3 This is the kitchen, and some of this dust has been combined with a thin layer of grease. Use a paper towel sprayed with window cleaner to cut through this dirt.

4 Be sure not to forget the windowsills.

5 Wipe off fingerprints on walls, light switches, the fronts of cupboards and drawers (don't forget the handles), and all major appliances as you circumnavigate the kitchen.

The Wall Wipe-Down

Kitchen walls not only receive abuse from splattered spaghetti, tiny colored handprints, and chunky chocolate splotches, they seem to suck up grease and grime just by being situated in the kitchen. The steam from boiling pots and running hot water acts almost like glue attaching particles that float through the air to everything in it's path.

Window cleaner or a small amount of detergent on a paper towel, dampened rag, or sponge will do the trick for getting most stains off pained walls. (I still like paper towels the best.) A really tough stain can be removed from white walls with a small amount of soft bleaching cleanser on a sponge. Test this cleaning method in a remote corner, if you want to try it on paint that is other than white. If your kitchen is wallpapered, here are a few tips for getting rid of marks, stains, rips, and dents:

- Try a soft eraser to remove mysterious marks and dirt; use it gently, being sure not to tear the paper. If that doesn't work, try the same gentle strokes, but with a piece of white bread.

A COMPLETE WASTE OF TIME

The Three Worst Things To Do with the Top of the Refrigerator:

1. Store items on it that you want to stay free of dust, grease, and grime.

2. Store items on it that you don't use often—you'll never remember where you put them.

3. Add a new item by sliding what's already up there back and assuming that if you don't hear a crash, nothing has fallen off and gotten stuck behind it.

If your kitchen table and chairs sit in tight quarters very close to the wall, install a chair rail to prevent the chairs from banging against the wall every time someone stands up.

- For unsightly grease spots, place a brown lunch bag or a piece of a brown grocery bag over the stain and press the area with a warm iron for a few seconds. The heat will absorb the grease onto the brown paper.

- In my home, the kitchen table sits very near the wall. If you're not careful when you get up, the chair can knock into the wall. The end result is that the wallpaper gets dented and nicked. If you're like me and don't want to put up a chair rail, it's simple to repair the dents.

The design on my kitchen paper is ivy, weaving its way over the walls. Here's a trick that my wallpaper hanger taught me. To replace a damaged leaf, I just cut out a duplicate from the wallpaper I saved after it was originally hung. Using a small bit of wallpaper paste and an old kitchen knife, I paste the new leaf over the damaged one. You cannot see that anything has been repaired, but you can feel the change if you run your hand across the wall. I've never tried this on non-patterned paper, but you could do a test run.

If you notice smudges on the windows, this is a good time to get them. There's no need to clean the windows if they're not dirty.

Clean the Countertops

You'll need:

- Paper towels
- Sponge
- Window cleaner
- Kitchen spray cleaner
- Soft scrubbing cleanser

1 Start from the back, moving items out of the way, and work your way forward.

2 Spray window cleaner, or a kitchen spray cleaner, if you prefer and a swipe of a paper towel to clean it.

3 If you come across a stubborn stain, like the juice from fresh raspberries, try a little Soft Scrub on a sponge to clean the Formica®. You don't want to scratch the surface. If your countertops are white, try Soft Scrub with bleach. It works for me every time. Polished granite counter tops clean up quickly and easily. Marble absorbs stains. Some people feel that the food stains add charm and simply ignore them.

Buffing Up the Backsplash

You'll need:

- Paper towels
- Sponge
- Window cleaner
- Tile cleaner

A COMPLETE WASTE OF TIME

The Three Worst Things to Do with Cleanser with Bleach:

1. Not remove things, like cloth napkins, placemats, towels and clothing, from your cleaning path first. Bleached out patches on fabric cannot be removed.

2. Lean against the edge of the counter top or table while cleanser may still be wet. You might end up with an entire wardrobe of clothing that has waist high horizontal white stripe as an adornment.

3. Use it on wood furniture. The bleach will most likely remove any wood stain or finish.

Do Double Duty and clean the electric can opener while you're talking on the phone. Unplug it, lift the handle release, and pull the handle and wheel right off the housing. Soak this piece in soapy water. Spray the rest of the appliance with glass cleaner. Wipe the case and serrated wheel with a paper towel. A toothpick will get into the crevices and clean any hard to reach areas. (I know that this sounds like a rather anal task, but it can be a great release if you are talking to someone on the phone who really irritates you.) Remove the handle from the soapy water, rinse it, dry it, and re-attach it to the case.

1 If the backsplash is made of the same material as the countertop, clean them at the same time.

2 If the backsplash is tile, spray it with the same tile cleaner that you use in the bathroom, do the countertops, and then wipe the backsplash. The tile cleaner practically works by itself.

Abolishing Grime from Appliances

You'll need:

- Paper towels
- Sponge
- Window cleaner
- Kitchen cleanser
- Soft scrubbing cleanser
- Steel soap pad

1 Wipe the small appliances that you haven't hidden away in a cupboard.

2 For stubborn stains, use a scrubbing cleanser or soap pad.

Tackling the Table and Chairs

Sometimes I feel as though I am having a recurring nightmare about wiping off the kitchen table. I'll bet that there are some evenings alone, when I do this at least three times. Just when I think that everyone is moving to another room and that the kitchen is closed for the day,

Bingo, someone starts snacking, reading the newspaper, or talking on the phone and doodling.

If you have small children, the chairs might even get dirtier than the table. Food becomes compounded with footprints. Whether you sit at a counter on stools, at a butcher-block table on cane chairs, or at a laminate parson's table on molded plastic seats, they all need a cleaning.

You'll need:

- Paper towels
- Sponge
- Window cleaner
- Pine-scented cleanser
- Furniture polish

1. If there are only a few crumbs on the table, then spray and follow step 2 for washable tables and step 4 for wood. If there are mountains of crumbs, bring the garbage can over to the table, and using a paper towel, sweep the crumbs directly into the trash.

2. Spray the cleaner onto the rag, sponge, or towel. Avoid showering the solution directly onto the surface; you might end up spraying more than you want.

3. Wipe off the table. Either let it air dry or go over the table top with a dry paper towel.

4. Many wood tables have been treated so that they can be sponged off or sprayed with window cleaner type product. For pure wood tables, spray the wood polish onto the rag or towel.

A COMPLETE WASTE OF TIME

The Three Worst Things to Do with Cleanser:

1. Squirt window cleaner indiscriminately. Too much of a good thing can make a big dripping.

2. Add another dash of detergent—it doesn't mean cleaner, it means twelve more rinses to remove all the unneeded bubbles.

3. Use it on something that's already clean. If it's not dirty, don't clean it

If you don't keep the box of trash bags neaby, store extra plastic garbage bags right inside the kitchen garbage can. When the current bag is full, pull it out, tie it up, and then pull up the new clean bag that's sitting right in the bottom of the trash can. You can keep several fresh bags stored in this manner. (So no more excuses as to why there's garbage on the bottom of the trash can!)

Getting Rid of the Garbage

If you've followed the tip of placing extra bags in the bottom of the can, this should be a cinch. You'll need:

- Your trash can, complete with new bags on the bottom
- disinfectant spray (optional)

1 Tie up the full bag and take it out to the garage.

2 Pull up a new bag from the bottom of the can.

3 If the garbage odor has lingered, give a quick crop dusting of the disinfectant spray (preferably before you pull up the new bag).

Finishing Off with the Floor

The wide variety of flooring choices requires different types of cleaning products. Luckily manufacturers have taken notice of our life styles and realized that what we want is simple, fast, and easy. Even hardwood floors that have a coat of polyurethane can be damp-mopped without fear of hurting the wood. If you're not sure what cleaning products to use on your specific floor, take a sample to a store that specializes in flooring and ask.

You'll need:

- Vacuum or broom

- Bucket

- Sponge mop or mop vac

- Floor cleaner (There are various types of cleaners for different types of floors: Life O' Wood and Murphy Oil Soap diluted in water work on wood floors as well as vinyl tile. A pine cleaner in water does a nice job on ceramic tile. And Spic and Span cleans all finished floors.)

1 Sweep, vacuum, electric broom, or dust mop the floor.

2 If your floor cleaner needs to be dissolved in water, fill the bucket with warm water.

3 Add floor cleaner according to the directions on the box or bottle.

4 Wash the floor using a mop vac or water and cleaner on a sponge mop.

5 If the floor has a nice shine to it, but appears lifeless after you wash it, rinse it with clean water to remove any soap residue.

If the floor was not shiny when it was installed, it probably was never meant to be. (My kitchen floor is a vinyl that is meant to replicate porous tile, grouting and all. It was laid the same way you would lay a ceramic tile floor. At first it bothered me that it scratched easily and was dull, even after I washed it. But I realized that it's doing exactly what it's supposed to do. And I've gotten to love that look.)

QUICK 🞄 PAINLESS

A quick vacuuming may be all that your floor needs. If there is just one patch that needs to be washed, a wet paper towel will handle the spot cleaning. You might want to try my husband's back-saving method. When his basketball gets the better of him and his back is so sore that he cannot bend over, he wets a double thickness of paper towel, drops it onto the floor and does this little skating movement to clean up the mess. He only needs to bend over once to pick up the dirty towel.

Voilà! Finis! Congratulations. Enjoy it while you can, because it's almost time to walk the dog, and it's raining.

TRICKS OF THE TRADE FOR EASILY KEEPING IT CLEAN

Sit down, darling. We'll have coffee, a little something sweet. I'll share some shortcuts with you. These are tricks of the trade that I've picked up from keeping my ear to the ground, my eyes open, and my mah-jongg hand closed.

What's That Smell?

Here are a few tricks for keeping your kitchen smelling fresh and clean:

- An open box of baking soda or a sliced apple will remove odors from your refrigerator.
- Put citrus fruits, especially lemons, ice cubes made from vinegar, or baking soda down your disposal for a fresher scent.
- Use the exhaust fan while cooking.
- Light a candle when cooking fish. (This might also work for cabbage.)

Painless Peels

Do the following directly into the garbage with no pit stops:

- Scrape vegetables.
- Husk corn on the cob.
- Peel fruit rinds.

- Core apples.

- Seed cantaloupe and honeydew.

- Shell shrimp (and take it to the garbage immediately so that it won't sit around overnight and smell up your house).

- Shuck clams (ditto the above).

- Peel potatoes.

- Snap asparagus and green beans.

Get Those Pots Clean Without Any Elbow Grease

When there's more dinner burned onto the bottom of your pot than ends up on your plate, don't throw out the pot. Instead, try these potent pot-luck pointers.

- Use your dishwasher's pot scrubber setting.

- Fill the pot half full with water; bring the water to a boil, stirring with a wooden spoon until all of the food deposits are loosened.

- If the pot becomes stained, fill it with three table-spoons of vinegar and a pint of water. Boil until the stain loosens. Wash the pot in soap and water.

Take Your Head Out of the Oven!

Buying a self-cleaning oven is the optimum answer to eliminating this household chore. But if this is not in your plans:

- Prevent spills by placing a cookie sheet or a pan under casseroles or pies that may bubble over.

QUICK PAINLESS

Before using your pasta strainer, colander, cheese grater and the like, spray them with non-stick veg-etable spray. When you wash the accessories, the cheese and pasta remains won't get gooey from the hot water.

Need a second oven? Want an oven that has parts that you clean in the dishwasher? Then check out a portable convection oven. It's not only great when you have a lot of foods to cook at one time (like Thanksgiving), but also, when it comes to cleaning, it sure beats sticking your head in the oven.

- Line the bottom of your oven with aluminum foil. However, aluminum acts as a heat conductor, which has a tendency to cause the item in question to cook unevenly. There is also a possibility that the bottom of whatever you are preparing will burn, while leaving the inside not fully cooked. You may wish to remove the foil when you bake.

- Soak the oven shelves in ammonia to clean off any baked-on foodstuffs.

- Spray the oven the night before you plan on cleaning it with a lemon-scented oven cleaner. Put a piece of newspaper on the floor under the opened oven door to catch any drips. By the time you wake up in the morning, the cleaner has done its job. Wipe out the mess with damp paper towels. Have the garbage can handy so that you can drop the messy towels into the trash. (These cleaners are meant to work while you sleep. But if you've experienced waking up in the morning to ooze all over your kitchen floor, then try spraying less cleaner into the oven and sticking paper towels into the space where the door hinges are.)

Who am I kidding? This job stinks no matter how you look at it. I say pay more attention to prevention and you'll lessen the work.

Raunchy Refrigerators

I rarely have to clean my refrigerator because I follow a few simple rules. I offer you these tips:

- Wipe up spills when they happen, or as soon as you see them.

- Try to keep all leftovers in covered containers so that if they do grow mold before you can catch them, the stench won't permeate the entire refrigerator, and it won't stare you straight in the face.

- Tidy up and wipe off a shelf when you need the space to store the perishables from your grocery bags.

- Store cheeses tightly wrapped in plastic and then encased in a ziplock bag. It slows down the blue mold from forming.

- Eat out as often as possible.

When in Doubt, Grab the Vinegar

The number of uses for vinegar is amazing. It is an astringent. Its chemical nature allows it to cut through grease, dirt, and residue produced by such foods as coffee and tea. Be sure to rinse thoroughly to remove any aftertaste. Here are a few more to help you keep things clean:

- Vinegar cleans and disinfects a wooden cutting board.

- Vinegar cleans a teapot. Rinse thoroughly.

QUICK n' PAINLESS

Use a mixture of baking soda and water to clean off the shelves in the refrigerator. Simply remove the food from the fridge, sprinkle the shelves with baking soda, and wipe with a wet sponge. Not only is this cleaner combination great for removing stuck-on goop, but it's also odorless. So your fridge won't smell like ammonia!

- Run vinegar through the coffee maker to increase the flow and clean out the clogs.(Be sure to run clear water though the brew cycle at least 2 to 3 times or you're in for a surprise with the first cup of coffee!! Yuck!)

- Vinegar can be used to clean out a refrigerator.

- Boil ¼ cup vinegar and one cup of water in the microwave to deodorize the microwave oven and loosen spattered on food deposits.

Pat yourself on the back. What a sport! You really deserve to do something fun after all this. It's your choice. Do you prefer a quiet game of chess or a two-hour workout at the gym that's followed by a dip in the pool and quiet time in the sauna? What ever you choose...enjoy.

The Lazy Way

Getting Time on Your Side

	The Old Way	The Lazy Way
Cleaning the oven	60 minutes	10 minutes
Wiping up	10 minutes	3 minutes
Scrubbing pots	6 minutes	2 minutes
Doing the dishes	10 minutes	4 minutes
Washing the floor	12 minutes	5 minutes
Emptying the garbage	3 minutes	1 minute

Chapter
nine

Put the "Rest" Back in Restroom

Y ou may find this hard to believe, but I really don't mind cleaning the bathrooms. Or rather, I don't really mind keeping the bathrooms clean. There is a difference. Since I am not one to set aside one day a week to scrub any one room in my home, I'd rather keep things up, day to day. (I find it to be much less time consuming; no one chore becomes overwhelming.) Keeping the bathrooms clean is more about simple routines and habits than hours of scrubbing.

Much of my regimen developed naturally from the good number of idiosyncrasies that influence the way I do things. Some of them have inspired my best timesaving cleaning methods.

YOU NEED ELBOWROOM IN THE LOO, TOO

Very nice! You're really grasping this concept that the less clutter, the cleaner your home will appear and be (and the easier

Since you're spending time organizing your toilet articles and bathroom cleaning products anyway, why not kill two birds with one stone? Do the job with a garbage bag by your side. I'll bet that you can fill at least half of it with deodorants that are dried out, perfumes that you don't wear, and medicines that expired years ago.

to keep clean). Minimizing the items on top of the counter near your bathroom sink is an outstanding example of this theory. If you were to line up all of the bottles, cans, sprays, and lotions that reside within the four walls of an ordinary bathroom, you may be able to open your own drug store. In addition to the lotions and potions, you have to store all the bathroom cleaning supplies, as well as extra toilet tissue, boxes of facial tissue, drain cleaner, a toilet brush and, in case of emergency, a toilet plunger.

The space under the sink is very roomy, but poorly designed because of the pipe drain taking up so much room. You're going to have to adapt the space to meet your storage needs. Even though the pipes from the sink obtrude into part of this area, there is still plenty of room to install stacking bins, or baskets of various sizes, to contain and organize all the paraphernalia you need.

Depending upon the size and arrangement of your lavatory, there might be leeway for a small decorative unit, or a series of closed shelves to hold your belongings and keep them as organized and as accessible as possible.

Hair sprays, deodorant sprays, and the like get into the air and deposit a thin film of greasy dirt all over the room. You can't necessarily see it, but if you run your hand over top of the toilet tank after you've finished styling your hair, you can feel it. It will cover all the containers and doodads that are out and about, so if you hide your belongings behind closed doors, you'll lessen the amount of time you have to spend dusting and washing them. (Medicine cabinets were designed to take care of this problem, but not all homes and apartments have them, as they used to.)

Bathrooms with pedestal sinks have a compound problem. The sinks themselves are very attractive, but they provide no place whatsoever to stockpile your supplies. Hopefully, if your bathroom features a sink of this design, the room is also blessed with a roomy linen closet, a medicine cabinet, or an area big enough to fit a small dresser or a piece of furniture the size of a two-drawer filing cabinet.

If there's not enough floor space in your bathroom, what about using a section of the wall to hang a unit?

If you go shopping for a wall unit, look for one that:

- Has hinged or sliding doors.
- Is as big as possible.
- Fills the empty area without becoming unsightly.
- Has a good number of shelves that will make it as functional as possible.

Even within a wall unit, you'll probably need small boxes, baskets, or bins to keep the area more organized and clutter-free. They'll help you grab what you need a lot faster. Consider storing the following items in small containers:

- Bandages and first aid items
- Nail clippers, small scissors
- Emery boards, nail polishes, and other manicure needs
- Barrettes, bobby pins, and other hair clips and wraps

YOU'LL THANK YOURSELF LATER

When looking for a wall unit for a bathroom, you might want to avoid any that are secured to the wall by sticky strips or suction cups—not only will this type of support not hold a lot of weight, but also the steam from the shower will lessen their adhesiveness and you'll just end up with a big mess on the floor.

- Extra razors
- Aspirins, cold and flu medications, thermometer
- Bars of soap

Countertop Stuff

You're going to want to keep a few things on top of the counter, not only for convenience, but also to keep the bath from looking too sterile and cold. The trick is to try to keep the number of items to a minimum. This is the perfect spot for things you use every single day, like perfume, aftershave, and an attractive bottle of body lotion. (Some people find it handy to leave their medications and vitamins on top of the bathroom counter. If it makes you happy, do it.) Coordinated bathroom accessory sets (including soap dish, tissue box, toothbrush holder, etc.) add a uniform touch to your bathroom's appearance. Since everything is similar, the countertops look neater. A pretty, washable tray to hold your bottles will also assist in organizing countertop clutter.

I tend to keep my "they tend to look messy" items like toothbrushes and toothpaste under the sink and far from public view. I hate the way a wet, just used toothbrush drips onto the counter. Whichever way you want to go, buy washable accessories. They will make your life easier in the long run.

Speed Reading

Bathrooms are not just for washing and flushing anymore. They have become additional living spaces. There are some terrific organizing tools that you can buy to keep all of your sundries in their place and out of the way. If this room doubles as a library, here are a few options for you to look into depending on the size and make-up of your bathroom:

- There are clever magazine racks that fit over the back tank of the toilet and hold at least a half-dozen volumes. If you purchase one of these racks, I suggest that you buy one that is constructed from plastic coated wire. They don't seem to gather too much grime. If a little dust gathers, swish it with your feather duster or spray some window cleaner onto a paper towel and wipe the dirt away. If you'd rather give the rack a good swift spritz, be sure to remove the magazines first.

- In larger bathrooms, consider using the style of magazine rack that sits on the floor. You know, the same kind that you would buy for the family room. When the magazines start to overflow the rack, sort them out while you're sitting on the throne. (I'm not sure if it's appropriate to say "do double duty" in this instance.)

- You may choose to hang a magazine rack on your bathroom wall. If you like a clean, contemporary, industrial look, there are several to choose from in various catalogs that specialize in bathroom fixtures, as well as home décor, such as Pottery Barn. (If your wall is tile, be sure that you know exactly where you want to hang it before you drill any holes. Tile is harder to repair than drywall.)

A COMPLETE WASTE OF TIME

The Three Worst Things to Do with Towels:

1. Leave them in a wet heap on the floor.

2. Hang them over the top of the shower curtain rod to dry, creating clutter.

3. Delegate the towel racks for the "for show" towels, and hide the usable towels in the linen closet.

Consider buying a black scale. It will show a little dust, but not heavy-duty dirt. A swipe with a static or feather duster removes most of the debris. A wet tissue smoothed across the top of the scale eliminates the rest of the dirt. Then toss the tissue into the toilet.

GO, JOHNNY, GO! HIGH-SPEED CLEANING

Cleaning the bathroom doesn't have to be draining. So get rid of that sinking feeling! We'll flush it out in no time.

Everything You Need Is Right Here

All the cleaning supplies you'll need should be stored right underneath the bathroom sink. Let's just list them again:

- Floor cleaning product
- Bleaching cleanser
- Toilet bowl cleanser
- Mildew cleaner
- Soap scum cleaner
- Drain cleaner
- Toilet brush
- Window or mirror spray
- Paper towels
- Sponges
- Cotton swabs
- Toilet paper
- Facial tissue
- Hand soap

All of the supplies are in place. Everything is at hand and where you need it. Remember—convenience is one of the keys to shortcut success.

Once you get into a maintenance routine, your cleaning will be a breeze. What follows are actual patterns that I go through in order to save myself time and energy in the long run. If you don't believe me, ask anyone in my family. Ready, set, go.

Shower Shortcuts

Now, won't you please join me in the shower? (Don't worry, this is G-rated.) And here we observe an age-old problem. What do you do with all of the bottles, razors, shaving creams, soaps, shampoos, conditioners, back scrubber, sponges, washcloths, and so on that you cannot do without? Even if your shower stall comes with a ledge or two, these projections always seem to be too small to fit what you intend to put on them, like the razors that keep slipping off and falling onto the shower or tub floor.

My suggestion: buy a shower caddy. These terrific gizmos come in various shapes and sizes. Look for one that will fit all of the different sized bottles that you use. Many caddies also come with hooks that are perfect to hold a back scrubber or loofah. The caddy fits over the showerhead and is held in place by a plastic anchor. There are usually one or two suction cups that snap on vertically and hold the device securely against the shower wall. And you never have to clean the caddy or the items that you store on it. The shower does it for you.

Some shower caddies have built-in soap dishes, which are very nice, since they don't seem to build up with soap scum. Our shower has a tile soap dish built into the wall.

QUICK n PAINLESS

With a tissue, remove any hair that ends up in the sink before the water takes it down the drain. One or two hairs will eventually accumulate into big globs and plug up the works.

It's very handy, is at the right height, and looks nice.
However, if you set the bar of soap in it, the wet soap
sticks to, and then dries on, the tile soap dish and creates
the deadly, hard-to-clean dulling soap scum. Yuck! There
are two resolutions to this problem:

1. Buy only liquid soap that comes in a plastic bottle
   that sets on your shower caddy.

2. Buy a simple plastic soap tray that fits right on the
   tile soap dish. I've always bought the rectangular-
   shaped soap trays. They seem to snuggle into the
   dish more comfortably than the round ones. These
   trays have little prongs that hold the slippery soap
   where it belongs.

Resplendent Restroom Rituals

To get the bathroom-cleaning job done with as little
effort as possible, I have little rituals that I go through
every day. Follow these simple steps and you'll put the
"rest" back into the word "restroom" in no time.

Stalling in the Shower

I don't know about you, but my mornings begin with a
shower. I cannot face the day or myself without this
refreshing picker-upper. The next eight steps will swiftly
cleanse both you and your shower.

Cleaning the Shower

You'll need:

- Sponge

- Cleaner such as Clean Shower, a soap scum remover, or a mildew remover

1 If you have a bathroom fan, now is the time turn it on.

2 If you have a bathroom window, you may wish to open it a crack. (I like to open the bathroom window more than a crack. It drives my husband crazy. I don't know why he lets those few flakes of snow that sometimes blow in bother him so much.)

3 Once you are clean from head to toe, rinse out the soap tray. Rinse the soap off a little bit. Then replace the pronged soap dish to its spot in the shower stall and put the soap back.

4 About once a week, take the plastic bottles of shampoo and bath-and-body-gel out of the caddy and run them under the water. This will remove any caked-on soap around the spouts and keep the liquids flowing easily.

5 If you're stepping out of a tub shower with a shower curtain, push it back for a few minutes. If you have a stall shower, leave the door ajar to permit the steam and moisture to discharge itself into the room. You turned on the fan or opened the window before you started your shower routine, so, the mist will diminish quite quickly. By drying out and cooling off the shower, and keeping fresh air circulating inside these closed quarters, you're fighting off

QUICK n PAINLESS

About once a week, before exiting the shower, grab the sponge that you keep on one of the caddy's shelves and quickly wipe the tile or the molded plastic walls. If you have a stall shower, a quick swipe to the inside of the glass doors will help the shower dry out faster and will eliminate some of the water spots and streaking.

the mold and mildew that loves to cling to the grout around the tile and on the plastic shower curtain liner.

6 Before you make your final exit, spray the shower area with either a soap scum, mildew cleanser, or one of the newer shower products that if used daily eliminate cleaning your shower entirely. And then walk away. The next time you run the water to heat up the shower, the cleanser washes away and you step into a sparkling clean stall or tub.

7 Sometimes black deposits appear out of nowhere. You can also handle this annoyance without any effort:

- Spray the tub or shower (#6 above)

- Squeeze a soft scouring product containing bleach onto the black marks. Then walk away. The next time you run the water, the white cleanser will be swept down the drain along with the black splotches. In fact, I don't think that you could have gotten the floor to sparkle like that no matter how long you scrubbed it.

8 When the shower seems relatively dry, shut the door, or fully extend the curtain. Your bathroom looks as neat as a pin.

Once-a-Week Rituals (or When Applicable)

Rub-a-Dub-Dub, Let's Not Forget the Tub

We cannot leave this section without mentioning bathtubs, standard and whirlpool. We all love bubble baths—they're a time to relax and forget the stresses of life. However, courtesy requires that the bather clean out the tub when finished in order to prepare for the next occupant. Unlike the shower, the tub is difficult to wash down completely while you're in it. Truth is, the particles of dirt that you have just scrubbed off your body are floating in the water in which you are now sitting. (Takes some of the luxury out of it, huh?) But, here are a few tips for moving this process along:

Cleaning the Tub

Bubble baths are fun, aren't they? Don't you just love to choose the bath oil fragrance that matches the mood that you're in? It feels so good to slide into the warm water and luxuriate in the multitude of bubbles. The day's tensions just melt away. As you slip out of the tub and wrap yourself in a warm fluffy towel, you turn to find the tub filled with gook!

Why not give these tips a try the next time you bathe:

1. Let the water start to drain out of the tub while you're still in it.

2. Have a sponge handy and wipe the tub at the high-water mark. If a ring-around-the-tub is going to collect, this will be the place. (Be sure that the sponge you clean with has a completely different look and color from the sponge that you may use to wash your body.)

3. Assist the water and bubbles down the drain, using the sponge as a pusher to move them along. Turn on the shower to assist you in this step. (My husband stays right in the tub during this last process. He stands and lets the shower take the last particles of soap off his body, as well.)

YOU'LL THANK YOURSELF LATER

Luxuriating in a bath piled high with bubbles is one of the ultimate images of relaxation. Removing those bubbles from the tub after your bath is a nightmare. Whenever you pour soap into water, keep in mind the adage "less is more."

To eliminate the gross gunk that accumulates in the bottom of the toothbrush holder and then drips onto the countertop, find something that's washable and big enough to hold all the bathroom occupants' toothbrushes and toothpaste. Instead of dangling the brushes from the holder in the backsplash, hide the toothbrush holder under the sink (away from the cleaning supplies) or in an enclosed cabinet— out of the way, and out of sight.

4 Spray with a cleanser that removes soap scum to eliminate any grime, soap sediment, or bath oil residue that clings.

5 One more quick rinse to remove any tiny particles of grit, and you're finished. Let the tub air dry.

Bathing Countertop Accouterments

Next to our bathroom sink, we keep a box of tissues in a decorative holder, a small vase-like receptacle for my cosmetic brushes, a soap dish, two bottles of perfume , and a bottle of aftershave. All of these items can stand to get wet without being ruined. You may have different items on your bath countertop, but, as long as they're washable, you should be able to clean them the same way. This may sound tedious, but it's really no big deal. **About once a week:**

Cleaning Off the Counter

You'll need:

- Paper towels
- Sponge
- Soft scrubbing cleanser with bleach
- Window cleaner

1 Run any bottles under hot water to quickly remove any of the debris that settled from sprays and lint from the hair dryer. The moisture that accumulates after you shower invites dirt to adhere to anything unenclosed.

2 Slip off the tissue holder from the tissue box and give it a speedy rinse.

3. Rinse off any other containers, jars, or bottles you may have on the counter. If you've mastered the "lazy way," you use only washable pieces on the countertop.

4. You know, from a hygienic standpoint, it's important to wash off your cosmetic brushes at least once a week. It takes no time to add this to your quick rinse-off cleaning action. Just let the brushes drip dry in the receptacle that holds them. Your face will be glad you did.

5. Then on some Sunday morning, while you are brushing your teeth and contemplating some earth-shaking story on the front page of the morning paper, run the toothbrush holder, brushes, toothpaste, and all under hot water until all the dried paste disappears. Drip it dry, of course. No hassle, no fuss, no mess.

6. Add a little more spit and polish to swabbing off the countertop. A little soft cleanser on a damp sponge takes care of that stain in a flash. On most mornings, just a damp sponge or sprits of window cleaner and then a swipe with a paper towel answers all my cleaning needs.

7. If you have children, a plastic bathroom cup dispenser and disposable cups are the safest and most hygienic route. If this is strictly an adult bathroom, put your porcelain cup into the dishwasher once a week.

8. Run your soap dish under hot water every few days to melt away soap residue.

9. Plastic soap dispensers also need a hot shower about once every week.

That's all there is to it. I wouldn't think of drying anything. There are a lot more things than a few water spots to worry about.

QUICK ɪɴ PAINLESS

Years ago, I came across what I think is one of the greatest soap dishes ever invented. It's made of bamboo. So, when the soap sticks and builds up soap scum, all you have to do is run the dish under hot water or let it soak a few minutes in the sink. The soap melts away and the soap dish is in perfect condition.

If you insist on wiping the mirror to defog it, here's a helpful hint. Hot water will defog the mirror; cold water will make it fog up all over again. It works on the same principle as the in-shower shaving mirrors. So if you do wipe your mirror down, run your towel in hot water.

Mirror, Mirror on the Wall

Don't touch that foggy mirror! You'll just streak it and then you'll have to clean it. How do you quickly alleviate mirror moisture?

- Turn on the fan before going into the shower.

- Open the window a crack (or more if you are in the middle of a hot flash or a pregnancy) before stepping into the shower stall.

- Open the bathroom door a crack (or all the way if you're home alone or don't care who sees you) to let cool air flow into the bathroom.

- Turn your hair dryer on and aim it at the mirror.

- If you have a medicine cabinet with sliding mirrored doors, you can open one side before you shower. When you step out, pull out the door that was tucked behind the other one and it's completely fog-free.

Toilet Training

There's little that you can do to make cleaning the toilet a pleasant experience. A tolerable experience, yes, but not enjoyable. Let's just get it over and done with, the faster the better. If you quickly wipe the toilet off once a week, the dirt and grime will not build up. This can really be a cinch.

Cleaning the Toilet

You'll need:

- Window cleaner
- Paper towels
- Toilet cleanser
- Toilet brush

1 Using window cleaner, spray the toilet from every side:

- Seat—don't forget to lift it up to get underneath
- Seat cover
- Tank
- Base

2 Grab a paper towel and rapidly swab off the cleaning liquid. That's all there is to cleaning the toilet fixture.

3 The inside of the toilet bowl does not have to be swished with the toilet brush every day. In fact, if you use the type of toilet bowl cleaner that you drop or hang inside the tank, the bowl cleans itself with every flush. Once in a while, every bowl needs a little extra help. That's when you brush. There are so many products on the market to assist you in performing this job. Some cleansers squirt, some spray, and some dribble. Choose your weapon. You do need a brush to swish things around, but that's about it. Like anything else in your home, the longer you ignore it, the dirtier it gets.

IF YOU'RE SO
INCLINED

If the sight of a toilet brush makes you bristle, consider buying one that comes with a decorative holder. The head of the brush sits in a tray that acts as the base. The handle can be anything from a duck to a cartoon character. You can even get a very simple, colored holder to match your bathroom's décor. I can't promise you it will make cleaning the toilet more fun, but it will look better.

Face Those Floors with a Smile

Is there any fine and fast way to approach cleaning your bathroom floor without making yourself crazy? I think so. As with everything else that we talked about, meet the bathroom floor straight on. If you can't manage a smile, try a little grimace. If this is your master bath, what possibly could have fallen to the floor in less than an hour's time? Once a week should suffice for this cleaning chore.

- **Hair:** Some of us may be dropping more strands than others.

- **Stickums:** This is similar to those little bugs that people refer to as no-see-ums. It's all that goo that collects all over everything. It's derived from deodorant and hair sprays, combined with the natural lint and dust that float around and are compounded by the warm burst from your hair dryer. Gritty residue is not necessarily noticeable to the naked eye, but your hands and bare feet recognize it immediately.

- **Lint** from tissues.

- **Makeup:** blush and eyeshadow powder, once floating in the air, has finally settled onto the floor.

- **Deposits** from something that fell from the counter or was dropped and scattered onto the floor.

This may not sound like a lot, but when all combined, it sure makes for an unsightly mess.

Cleaning the floor is a great little job for a Dust Buster or an electric broom, if they are handy.

A Creative Way to Flashy Floors

Here's an additional idea, not strictly kosher, but easy.

You'll need:

- Hairdryer
- Toilet paper
- Toilet

1. When you finish blowing your hair dry, move the bathroom throw rugs aside.

2. Aim the dryer toward the floor and blow the debris toward a corner.

3. Wet a piece of toilet paper, pick up the little bundle of hair and other litter, and toss the paper onto the toilet.

4. Flush. The end.

I'm not saying that you're never going to have to actually mop the floor; about once a week should be enough for that. This straightening up concept goes back to the premise that any room will stay clean if you deal with the small stuff regularly.

Do you have dark stains running around the baseboard and corners of your bathroom floor? Those are not stains. Those are accumulations of hair and dust. Even if the rest of the floor is as clean as a whistle, these dark globs make the entire floor appear dirty. And they're so easy to get rid of!

QUICK ᴖ PAINLESS

If you have the room and a spare plug, a Dust Buster is a great little appliance to keep near the bathroom. You'll be surprised how often you'll use it.

If you decide to try spraying your floor with a bleach product, do remember to remove your towels and rugs from the area. You may not notice that some of the spray hit the towels as you backed out of the room, but you definitely will see it when you return. The little bleached out dots, in a variety of sizes, do not add character to your décor.

Cleaning Stubborn Floor Tile Grime

Here's another one of my floor cleaning tricks. You know about all the cleaning products that tout how quickly and easily they work on tile to keep it clean without any muss or fuss. Why should you relegate this cleaner only to wall tile, particularly wall tile within your tub or shower area? The tile and grout get pretty raunchy on the floor, as well.

You'll need:

■ Tile mildew remover spray with bleach.

1 Remove the towels and rugs from the bathroom.

2 Squirt the floor with one of the tile cleaners that contains bleach. (You might also try Clean Shower.)

3 Back out of the room, squirting as you go.

4 That evening, when you come home from work, mop the floor with nothing but water. It really works. The grout is whiter than it was in the morning.

LILLIPUTIAN LAVATORIES

We must give some special notice to the bathrooms whose occupants are less than 30 inches tall. Here's to the tots, the terrible twos, and the toddler toilet trainees.

They may not all be straight shooters, but they do know how to make a room their own.

A kids' bathroom is a little more difficult to keep intact. It's not just a few magazines that you have to find places for, it's the trucks, ducks, and squeaky toys. It's the potty seat, the step stool, and the big boy's soap dish.

Tidying for the Tikes

Uncluttering this bathroom is a little more challenging, and maybe you need to be somewhat creative. You cannot hide the potty seat or the step stool in a cupboard or behind a plant. That's just defeating the purpose. They must have their prominent position next to the toilet. But you can try some of these tidying-up ideas:

- Towel racks hung at nursery-school height, or a junior-sized coat rack, will encourage the kids to hang their own towels. (If Daddy has a problem following through when it comes to hanging up his towel, you may have to train him first.)

- A small basket will store *Pat the Bunny* and other animal stories. Many of the books are waterproof, so you need not worry if they end up in the toilet bowl. But please don't flush.

- Put all of the tub toys in a string bag and hang the bag from the bathtub faucet. Close the shower curtain for privacy.

- The countertop should probably be free from most types of items. A box of tissues is okay. This is one

QUICK n' PAINLESS

Clean your porcelain sink by pulling up the drain stop and filling the sink with $1/2$ cup of bleach and hot water. Let the compound soak for about one hour. Be sure that the bathroom is ventilated, and the kids don't go near it.

time when a toothbrush and toothpaste holder is worthy of prominence.

- For convenience, it's still a good idea to keep all of the cleaning supplies for this bathroom inside the room. You do need to take some precautions, however. If you stockpile the items under the bathroom sink, be sure to buy the childproof hooks to keep little hands and mouths away from dangerous chemicals. If you have a linen closet in the bathroom, the top shelf would be an even better storage spot. A lock on this door wouldn't hurt either.

Lollygagging in the Lav

The kids bathroom is a great place to do Double Duty. You know, that's the "Can you walk and chew gum at the same time?" concept that we talked about in Chapter 4. Try a few of these simultaneous scenarios the next time you find yourself in the children's loo:

1. While they're playing in the bath

   - Clean out a drawer.
   - Wipe down the potty seat.
   - Rinse out the toothbrush holder.
   - Wipe off the countertops.

2. While they're sitting on the potty

   - Wash out the tub.
   - Wipe off the light fixture.
   - Check the ceiling for cobwebs.

IF YOU'RE SO INCLINED

If you just can't stand the soap build-up from around the metal rim of the bathroom sink, there's a simple way to clean it. A quick squirt with any liquid will dampen the area and a toothpick will remove the scum.

- Work with them to sort out some of their bathroom books.
- Wipe off any spots on the mirror.
- Plan a party to celebrate your new approach to house cleaning.
- Reread *War and Peace*.

Getting Time On Your Side

	The Old Way	The Lazy Way
Scrubbing the toilet bowl	6 minutes	2 minutes
Demildewing the shower	15 minutes	1 minute
Straightening up for company	10 minutes	2 minutes
Cleaning the kid's bathroom	15 minutes	8 minutes
Cleaning out the bathtub	6 minutes	3 minutes
Finding the Super Heroes Bandages	4 minutes	1 minute

ten

No-Bother Boudoirs

It's interesting that, as the world becomes more automated and high tech, features that were standard necessities in most homes years ago are being reintroduced as accessories for gracious living. Look at the many homes that are now being built with back staircases, more than one fireplace, a great room instead of a living room and family room, a den that is reminiscent of the library of yesteryear, and large wonderful walk-in pantries.

The bedroom's role has expanded far beyond just a place to sleep. It has become a haven for unwinding from the stresses and strains of life's daily activities. You watch TV, read, talk on the phone, catch up on office work, exercise, play games with the kids, and watch old movies while munching on a big buttered bowl of popcorn. All this activity can cause quite a mess!

CLUTTER, CLUTTER EVERYWHERE AND NOT A SPOT TO SIT

There are some bedrooms that have the square footage to handle entertainment centers, exercise equipment, bookcases

If you only have a few wrinkles and creases in your suit and you don't want to go through the whole process of taking out the iron and ironing board, try hanging it in the bathroom while you shower. The steam will act as a pressing agent. Be cautious with silk and some rayon, though; water spots can stain your garment. On fabrics such as cotton, you can remove wrinkles by hanging your garment and then spraying it lightly with water just to dampen. Try running your fingers over the pants' leg creases.

and office furniture, and a comfortable easy chair. And then there are homes that hold all of the above in a 9' x 12' area. Let's play with the idea that the room that we're talking about is bigger than the size of your dining room area rug, but smaller than the master suite in the Taj Mahal. Okay, so not the Taj Mahal. Would you accept 17' x 20'? Just adapt these ideas to your own bedroom size. First we'll organize the clutter and then we'll clean the room.

Not only will hanging up and putting away your clothes make the bedroom look cleaner, it can also save you time, money, and even embarrassment.

Start with the Clothes

Instead Of:	Try This:
Dropping your clothes where you take them off.	Hanging them back in the closet.
Throwing your clothes over the back of the chair.	Folding them and putting them back in their proper drawer.
Hanging your clothes on the door stop on top of the door.	Throwing them into the dirty clothes hamper or down the chute.
Draping your clothes half way in and half way out of the laundry hamper.	Placing them on top of the pile with the rest of the clothing that has "go to the cleaners" written all over it.

Besides a neater looking room, there are other benefits of putting your clothes away:

- Some of the wrinkles will hang out before you wear the clothing again, so you'll save the time you would have spent pressing it or taking it to the cleaners. And just think of all the money you'll save on your dry cleaning bill!

- If you'd refolded your sweater and repositioned it on the shelf from whence it came, that cockeyed crease down the front would never have been there in the first place. And people wouldn't have been looking at you all day thinking that you just rolled out of bed.

- If you took your clean clothes that you piled on the floor, and had hung them in the closet, they would have remained clean and could have been worn, again.

- If your shoes are put away in pairs, either in their original boxes or on the shoe tree, instead of thrown on the floor and under the bed, you would not have arrived at the office this morning wearing a navy blue wedgie on your left foot and a classic black pump on your right. (Didn't the limp clue you in at all?)

- And you would not have missed the train if you had removed your black belt from your pant loops and hung it on the "belt" hook you installed. It's the dumping your pants on the floor, and covering them with a shirt, sweater, tie, jacket, and wet workout

YOU'LL THANK YOURSELF LATER

Instead of disposing of the clothes that you are wearing onto the floor, a chair, the bed, or on top of the dresser, hang them up or throw in the hamper as soon as you take them off.

clothes that cost you that account this morning, not your breathless presentation.

- And if your spouse looks at *your* clutter with disdain and no longer picks up your piles but walks around them, keep in mind that legal fees cost a bundle.

If you've become hooked on closets, you may want to flip to Chapter 12. It's full of detailed advice on how to organize clothes closets and drawers to keep them, and your clothing, tidy.

Moving Right Along to Reading Material

It's so comfortable to snuggle into the covers, propped against mounds of pillows, to peruse a juicy murder mystery, this week's news magazine, your favorite female fashion journal, or the male version of a fashion periodical—the swimsuit edition of *Sports Illustrated.* The piles of books and magazines seem to grow before your very eyes. You are so busy with your day-to-day activities that you just can't seem to keep up with the ever-growing piles of catalogs, monthly mags, and "must reads." And there are all those articles, pictures, and recipes that you really want to copy or cut out to file away for future use. Here are a few suggestions for organizing the mile-high pile of periodicals.

- The traditional magazine rack in which you keep your most recent cache: Buy one for the bedroom to keep your favorite late night periodicals close at hand.

- Baskets, boxes and bins that we used in Chapter 6. Since this is your bedroom, choose containers that complement your color scheme and taste. For example, you could stack decorated hat boxes in a barren corner.

- A magazine-filled basket would add interest to the barren area underneath the side table that sits next to the chair and ottoman near the window.

- Utilize areas of your bookshelves to stack groups of magazines horizontally, spine-side facing out. Keep issues of the same magazine together for easy access and a neat appearance.

If you have oodles of magazines to deal with in the bedroom, then it's time to sort and trash. We've been finding little niches for periodicals all over the house: in the hall, living room, family room, and even the bathroom. There are probably issues of cooking and wine publications among the cookbooks in your kitchen. If the piles in the bedroom are hip high, reconcile yourself to the fact that you are never going to read them all, and cull those you want to keep there.

Next Stop, Nightstands

Let's flip through the decorating books once more. Aren't the bedrooms beautiful? Did you get a load of some of the nightstands? They work so well with the balance and design of the rest of the room. Look at that one; isn't it stunning? A simple slab of one inch beveled

IF YOU'RE SO
INCLINED

If there are certain titles that you cannot part with, or feel that they will someday be collector's items or have some other historic significance, why not purchase magazine binders? You can store about a dozen of the same title inside a single binder. The journals can occupy an area on a bookshelf without being in danger of falling over. You may decide to keep only individual issues that are of interest instead of full volumes. Even so, the binders serve a useful purpose.

glass balanced on top of a pair of semi-circular wrought iron legs. Or look at that one. The table top sits on a huge birdhouse! Gracing the piece is a vase holding one perfect calla lily and a first-edition leather-bound volume of sonnets. Where is the box of tissues? What happened to the alarm clock, the Sunday crossword puzzle, the bowl of popcorn, the extra pair of reading glasses, and the fingerprints? Hello?! Does anyone live here?

Nine times out of 10, I am the first one to select form over function. But that has to do with shoes, not night tables. If my husband and I had to grade our bedroom set, we'd give the size of the bed a "B," the mattress an "A," and the nightstands a "D-." The nightstands were a major mistake. Each unit consists of a drawer and two open shelves. (Bells should be going off in your head at this statement. Open shelves? Very dumb move!) I realize now that it doesn't matter how neat a person is, open shelves are a clutterer's catastrophe waiting to happen and a dust bunny's dream.

The shelves in question are so close to the ground that they collect dust every time you walk by them and every time you vacuum. The only way to guarantee their continued cleanliness is to remove the contents once a week, scour each item thoroughly, and then wipe out the shelves, being sure to get into the corners where dirt can collect. If I didn't have a headache before, I have one now.

I'm stuck with this situation for the time being, but I'm already planning our next nightstand purchase. Here are a few blueprints for a terrific bedside table:

YOU'LL THANK YOURSELF LATER

Use small boxes to store photos that are waiting for an album or all the extra buttons that come with new clothes. At least you'll know where they are when you need them.

- As wide a piece of furniture as will fit next to each side of the bed.

- Three deep drawers seem ideal.

- A top deep enough to hold a lamp, a telephone, and an alarm clock.

- Space to rest a drink, a snack, a book, a magazine, and a thick catalog, without having to rearrange everything.

- A top made of a material that is resistant to spills. Or treat the surface with polyurethane or have it fitted with a half-inch thick piece of glass.

- Night tables that don't necessarily match, but look well together and fit into the general room décor.

Since bedrooms have become havens for relaxation and sanctuaries from daily chaos, we tend to surround ourselves with objects that once were kept in other rooms of the house, like extra batteries and extension cords

If you have the space and you're in the market for new bedroom furniture, you may wish to look into two small three-drawer dressers rather than conventional nightstands. Be sure that these chests are of a convenient height, and a width that will fit the space. If you can use a chest that is wider than a standard night table, the possibilities for storage are expanded even further.

Modular units that stack and store are another alternative to your bedside table dilemma. And if you're feeling creative, some magazines present some very inventive and attractive ways to create night table units with a

QUICK ᴍ PAINLESS

Save a drawer in your nightstand to stash items that you don't want to get out of bed for or leave the confines of your room to retrieve. Light bulbs, batteries, matches, hard candy, a magnifying glass, and an extension cord may be a few of your choices. (Boy, you are lazy!)

good amount of storage area. For instance, try turning stackable wooden storage crates into a roomy and decorative piece of furniture. Pile two crates, one on top of the other, next to your bed. Top the two off with a piece of plywood that has been cut into a circle, a square, or a rectangle larger than the crate itself. (Since these are crates, they have slats on all sides and are not perfectly flat. Therefore, you need to create a level surface.) A floor length piece of fabric, fashioned into a tablecloth, covers all the mishmash underneath. A piece of glass cut to fit the tabletop protects everything from accidental spills. This is a great and inexpensive alternative to making a major furniture purchase. A round, cloth-draped table on one side of the bed and a traditional nightstand or chest on the other is a very interesting, as well as utilitarian, approach to hiding clutter. However, there are a few drawbacks to this bedside set up:

- Every time you need something in the crates, you have to lift the table skirt.
- Since there are slats in the crates, you will want to employ the tried and true boxes and baskets to prevent items from, literally, falling through the cracks.
- The glass top is easy to clean, but the table skirt tends to collect dust. It will need regular vacuuming, and a cleaning and pressing from time to time.

That's Entertainment

Since TV sets are common components of bedroom décor, it makes sense that entertainment centers have

YOU'LL THANK YOURSELF LATER

If you are considering setting up this style of nightstand or end table, choose your fabric carefully. For effortless upkeep, you probably won't want a light color, a fabric that wrinkles easily, or a fabric like silk or rayon that can stain from water spills. There are some interesting fabrics on the market that are machine washable, need no ironing, and are meant to have the wrinkled look.

come to be included in bedroom furnishings. And a blessing it is, too! They hide all the wires that attach the TV to the VCR and both to the wall socket. You can close the cabinet doors on a multitude of potential disarray. In one nice closeted area you are able to conceal:

- A TV set
- The Sunday section of the newspaper with the weekly program listings
- A VCR
- Stacks of VCR tapes on which you have recorded your favorite shows
- Blank VCR tapes
- Movies that you've bought (or rented and just haven't gotten around to returning)
- An audio tape cassette player
- Audio tapes (musical and books on tape)
- CD player
- CDs

And don't think that you have to try to fit those big entertainment units into your 9' x 12' bedroom. There are small units designed specifically for this purpose.

Do you know about Fibber McGee's closet? On their radio show, Fibber and his wife Molly had a closet that she didn't want him to open. It was filled to the brim with Fibber's treasures. Of course, he did open the door, and everything poured out and the audience laughed hysterically. But I'll bet that it was Molly who had the last laugh. Until Fibber opened the closet door, everyone

thought that the room was as neat as a pin. No one could see what accumulations and clutter really were hidden behind those closed doors.

Got the picture? Keeping your treasures behind closed doors will foster the appearance of a neat and tidy room. If your video tapes are not neatly stacked, no one will see them. If you're saving every birthday card your kids ever gave you in your top dresser drawer, no one will see them. If you find it easiest to throw your clean underwear into a drawer rather than folding each piece, so be it. (It sure is better than leaving it in the center of the bedroom floor in the laundry basket.)

Have fun deciding how you're going to create your neat private space. There are so many different styles of furniture and chests, and in all different price ranges, to choose from. If a Mission-style cabinet doesn't look right in the bedroom, but you love it, it might be great for the family room, or the upstairs hall, or even possibly the kitchen. You may decide to choose a wicker trunk to hold all your sweaters. Just keep in mind that no matter what you pick, to keep the lid on it!

Benign Bookcases

You may not have the space for either a built-in bookcase or a freestanding one. If you don't, try to keep your bedroom reading material to a minimum. Only leave the books that are on your current reading list on your bedside table. The main advantage of a bookcase is to

IF YOU'RE SO INCLINED

Nothing in life, and especially in room decorating, is forever. When choosing a home entertainment center, consider a freestanding unit that can serve another purpose at a later time and place. Are the shelves adjustable? Can additional shelves be purchased and kept for a future metamorphosis? Is the unit installed with an optional wardrobe pole?

confirm the old adage "a place for everything and every-thing in its place."

TIDYING TIDBITS

Before we start straightening up, let's pop into the bath-room and grab the cleaning supplies that you need for the bedroom. Put them into the little handled basket for easy transportation.

- Feather duster
- Window or mirror spray
- Paper towels
- Sponges
- Cotton swabs
- Vacuum cleaner

It was such a good idea back in Chapter 6 to rearrange the big linen closet so that it can house a sec-ond vacuum cleaner and an electric broom, wasn't it? And, see, you really don't miss that half shelf where the paper towels are now stacked. It's worth a little closet squeeze not to have to go downstairs every time you want to pick up a little lint.

Let's discuss this bedroom-cleaning thing first in the light of what you can do every morning before you leave the house. The goal is to be able to come home and find your bedroom orderly. This will be quick and with very few steps.

A COMPLETE WASTE OF TIME

The Three Worst Snacks to Spill in the Bedroom

1. A carbonated drink—if you have a wood night table, it can eat away the finish.

2. Foods with a tomato base—they stain easily. The longer they sit, the harder they are to remove.

3. Snacks like potato chips and popcorn—they leave crumbs in hard to find spots, as well as grease stains.

Every Day:

1. Whether the most luxurious silk pajamas or the free T-shirt you got at the gym, hang your night clothes up on the hook you installed on the back of the bathroom door, or drop them into the drawer that you set aside for this purpose.

2. Put the half-eaten bags of fat-free potato chips, the empty bottle of water, and yesterday's half-read newspaper into the handled picnic hamper to be taken downstairs and put in the garbage. (Remember Chapter 6?) You can dump it on your way out of the house.

3. Put any reading material that you threw on the floor at lights-out back on the nightstand or a bookshelf.

4. Shut down the VCR. That movie wasn't that great; it really didn't matter that you fell asleep. Put the videocassette back in the drawer of the entertainment center.

5. No need to go around picking up clothes—your clothes are all hung up! (Hey, those organizing tips really do work.)

6. Last, but not least, let's make the bed. Now close your mouth; we'll wait until the color drains back into your face. This really is a no big deal project. Did you share your bed with anyone last night? Well, then, have your roomie get on one side of the bed, and you get on the other. Before you can say clean sheets, the task is finished.

Fitted sheets keep the bottom sheet in tact even through the most restless of nights. Yank up the top sheet; folding it over and tucking it under is a matter of preference. Pull up the quilt and toss on the throw pillows. That's it!

QUICK 𝗻 PAINLESS

Turn making the bed into a "nothing to it" occurrence. Just pull the comforter up to the top of the bed, (hiding your slept on sheets) and toss on a whole bunch of decorative pillows. (They are called "throw pillows," you know.) Your bed is ready for *Architectural Digest*.

Every Once in a While...

When your room needs a bit more than a quick pick-me-up, a few more steps are in order. Remember, if it's not dirty, don't clean it. But if it is:

1. Use your faithful feather/static duster. Start at the ceiling and work your way down the wall, grabbing the dust particles and stubbing out the little cobwebs as you go.

2. Squirt the pictures on the walls and the photos on the shelves with glass cleaner, wiping them off with a paper towel. You might find it easier to squirt the towel with the cleaner and then wipe the glass.

3. Your collectibles on the shelf are next. If a feather duster does the trick, don't bother stopping to spray and dry each perfume bottle.

4. As you pass the window, give it a spritz and a wipe wherever you see dirt or hand prints. It won't hurt to check the windowsill for soot.

5. Run the feather duster over the books.

6. Dust the bedside lamps, alarm clock, and the telephone.

7. Wipe off the tops of the night tables.

8. Be sure to check the fingerprints near the light switches. Wipe them off with the dampened paper towel.

9. Use the vacuum cleaner attachments and suck up dirt on the moldings, drapes, and baseboards.

YOU'LL THANK YOURSELF LATER

If it's cold season, use a disinfectant cleaner on the phone to help keep germs from being passed around.

YOU'LL THANK YOURSELF LATER

Peek under the bed
before you stick the
cleaning attachment
under there. You don't
want a sock, a free
weight, or the cat to
get sucked up. They're
buggers to remove,
especially the cat.

10 Change to the upholstery accessory attachment and go over the easy chair and ottoman. Plump up the throw pillows and be sure to cover that red wine stain. Refold the afghan that you used during your nap yesterday.

11 If your bedroom has hardwood floors and an area rug, use either an electric broom or a dust mop and sweep around the circumference of the room. Then grab your vacuum to pick up any lint on the rug. If your machine has a suction regulator, this is a good time to use it. If wall to wall is your carpet of choice, use the crevice attachment to do the circumference of the room, and then vacuum the rest.

12 Don't forget to use the wand attachment on the vacuum to suck out those dust bunnies under the bed.

NEED A FEW TIPS?

Arresting Aromas

Odors are not the most pleasant things to talk about. There are a few that creep up in the bedroom, and they're quite easy to eliminate:

- Spray your favorite perfume or aftershave on the light bulbs of your bedside lamps or recessed fixtures. Every time you turn on the lights, the heat distributes the aroma around the room. Mmmmm. Very nice.

- Set a small dish of white vinegar in a corner. It's a natural odor killer.

- Those "plug in" deodorizers are very effective. I like them because they work all the time, not just when you spray. It comes in little gel-like packets. You put the packet into its holder and plug it into an electrical socket. I like the ones that leave a naturally fresh odor the best.

- There are fragrances that you spray onto your sheets. They restore the linens to their pre-slept-in state.

- Fresh air is the finest room invigorator. If your room has cross ventilation you can create a wonderful airflow. Or leave one or more windows cracked during the day to turn stale air into a breath of fresh air.

Dressers and Drawers

If I had my druthers, I would prefer to have a small bedroom and a really big and roomy walk-in closet. I prefer built-ins to dressers. Each of us is unique in the way he or she wants to organize his or her belongings: Customization is the answer. But not everyone has the space or the means to build something to specification. The next best thing is to compartmentalize your drawers. You can do this by buying a variety of wire baskets or drawer organizers that are like little boxes and come in wood or plastic.

- Use a few baskets in your sock drawer to help organize the different colors and patterns of socks.

QUICK ⬤ PAINLESS

You'll enjoy your collectibles even more if you keep them somewhere they'll stay clean and still be able to be seen. Cabinets and etageres with glass doors are the perfect vehicle for displaying your treasures. Many even come wired for inside lighting. Store your collectibles in style.

- Use the baskets to keep the different shades of panty hose separated by color. It saves time when you're in a hurry and cannot determine whether the stockings are navy or black.

- Ladies can also divide bras and panties by color. No more mix and match.

- Keep scarves together in larger drawers. They won't crease if they're kept flat.

- Use the baskets to organize your jewelry drawer.

When you are finished straightening up the bedroom, a nice way to reward yourself is to take a nap. (But try not to wrinkle the sheets.)

The Lazy Way

Getting Time on Your Side

	The Old Way	The Lazy Way
Pressing wrinkles out of a suit	6 minutes	2 minutes
Getting the dirty clothes together for the wash	10 minutes	3 minutes
Vacuuming	6 minutes	2 minutes
Finding the flashlight you left right next to the bed	3 minutes	30 seconds
Looking for the catalog that had the perfect Xmas gift for Aunt Gertie	10 minutes	1 minute
Making the bed	3 minutes	1 minute

Fun and Games: The Children's Room

To make sure that we are all on the same page, let's agree on the ages of the children who live in this room. On the younger end, they should be older than two, because until they reach toddlerhood, the only messes that they make are when they spit up, don't keep everything in their diapers, and declare their independence by throwing all of their toys out of the crib. And on the older end, they should be less than pre-teen—that still sweet, adorable, and malleable stage, because, after that, they start spreading their wings, have their own ideas about room décor, and need their own space. At that point, even if they do invite you into their rooms, you'd rather not go.

ONE, TWO, BUCKLE MY SHOE: ORGANIZATION

The children's room is the room in which you can really put your organizational skills to work. Don't tell the kids that

If your kids are at the age where presenting them with several options will not result in "I want everything," share with them some of your decorating magazines and catalogs that feature children's rooms. Sit down with a cup of cocoa and a pad of paper, flip through the pages, and jot down ideas. And maybe since they're looking at photgraphs of rooms where there aren't any piles of clothes on the floor, coats thrown over chairs, and unmade beds, they'll be more inclined to keep their own room neat. (Well, we can always hope.)

I said this, but this space deserves the KISS principle (Keep It Simple, Stupid). The hidden agenda in this situation is that, eventually, you want to delegate the "pick it up and keep it tidy" process to the kids. If you can prove to them that straightening up their room is no big deal, you're more than halfway there.

Here are a few ideas to get you started. As your baby grows from toddler to preteen, room schemes also will evolve continually. Pick and choose those ideas that are age appropriate for the children in your home.

If you want to give your organizational initiative a fighting chance, ask your children to be part of the planning process.

1. Work together to sketch out a room plan. How should you arrange the room so that there is plenty of space to hold tea parties and build castles? Where will the bed go? On what wall should you store the toys?

2. Do you need shelves for Little League trophies?

3. Does the hamster need an area to himself, or will all of his gear fit onto one corner of the desk?

4. Can all the trucks be arranged together, or do the dump trucks have to be separated from the fire engines?

5. How much room do you need for the Beanie Babies?

Now it's time to go shopping. You can do this either at the mall or through a catalog. You may even want to start looking at catalogs, like The Right Start or the kids-only catalog from Lillian Vernon. Or the Sunday paper's advertising inserts. Often Target, K-Mart, and toy stores such as Toys 'R Us have great organizers and bins that are suitable for rough and tough children's rooms. They'll help you get a few ideas.

Five, Six, Pick Up Sticks: Toys First

One big closed toy box: Sounds like a great idea! Everything will be hidden from view. But what happens when the Tonka truck that Susie wants to play with is at the bottom of the box? You got it. Susie is forced to throw every other toy onto the floor as she works her way to the bottom of the toy chest to retrieve the truck. I think that there might be some better alternatives.

Let's make one thing clear: I am not a child safety expert. When shopping for any items for your child's room, stores specializing in these types of items will have salespeople who are knowledgeable in safety matters. There are also books available that are shoppers' guides for children's products. If you are not buying from a specialty store, be sure that the person you are taking to really knows his stuff! Safety is not something that is to be taken lightly.

IF YOU'RE SO INCLINED

Buy storage containers that will grow with your child. Shelves can be raised to various heights, and stackable plastic bins are great in a college dorm. To save time and energy, pack the bins at home with whatever they're going to hold in the dorm room.

- **Shelves:** That's a good idea. Attach them at a height that your child easily can reach. Watch where you place them, though. You don't want to have any corners sticking out that a little eye could run into. I put shelves up in my kids' rooms when they were small, and sat all the toys on the shelves at a prescribed distance from one another. But then I can be

When you choose shelves for your child's room, make sure they can withstand the elements: a spilled fish tank, abusive toys, pasting, painting, and Silly Puttying. Pick a material that is practical and heavy duty. If you can't scrub it, rub it, and tub it, then you don't want it.

a bit anal retentive, at times. If you have these tendencies, or if your child does, look at the next point.

▪ **Stackable, brightly colored, heavy-duty plastic bins**: a very good thought. Variety is the spice of life, so you may want to choose some bins with slats on the bottom and others that are solid. The little Fisher-Price people won't get lost if you store them in bins without openings at the bottom. And don't forget the thousand or more pieces of Legos.

Bins also make the cleaning-up process easier. When it's time to take down the castle, carry the bin to the edifice, and, brick by brick, toss the building blocks into it. When the project is finished, carry the bin back to where it was.

▪ **Stackable wire bins on wheels:** another storage option. Maybe you've seen these used in closets to store sweaters and the like. The units come in a variety of sizes. First, you put together a framed support that holds the baskets in place. This contraption has wheels on the bottom and tracks at various heights in which to slide the baskets. The hoppers are made of wire mesh and have open spaces on all sides. They're useful for storing books, stuffed animals, Beanie Babies, and other soft items ,and, later on when your child matures, can serve many other purposes.

▪ **Cabinets with doors and deep drawers** hide a multitude of clutter.

Put the **picnic hamper** to work, once again. This does not have to be a huge basket. Try a smaller size this time, one that your child can carry. Fill it with the treasures that your youngster is most attached to. When he goes to Bailey's house to play, he can grab his hamper and bring his favorite toys along. It also makes the departure from Bailey's house a lot easier. Everything gets put back into the hamper and taken to the car for the ride home.

Seven, Eight, Lay Them Straight: Clothes Are Next

Have you ever looked into the closet in a toddler's room? Hanging on the closet pole, on adorable little hangers, are teensy-weensy dresses, jump suits, jackets, and the like. (Of course, when the kids get a bit older and start dressing and undressing themselves, the closet won't look this cute and neat, especially if the rack is too high for the little tots to reach.) Below the clothing is four feet of empty space. What a waste! Utilize this space to your advantage.

While Amy Beth is tiny, keep the closet pole at adult height. Allocate one third of the space to the baby (and the rest to Mom and Dad. Shhhh. I won't tell Amy if you won't.).

1. Place one of the wheeled stacking bins in Amy's third of the space, right underneath her hanging items. Use the bins as you would a dresser.

QUICK n° PAINLESS

Set up a mini-hammock in your child's room and fill the net with all the stuffed animals. They'll look cute swinging there, they're easy to keep straightened, and they won't fall out.

QUICK ⟨n⟩ PAINLESS

2. Fill one basket with sleepers, one with over-alls and one-piece outfits, one with T-shirts and one with booties, socks, and shoes.

3. If there is already a dresser in the room, use the bins to store the clothes that the baby has outgrown, or outfits that he has not yet grown into.

4. Keep the bins organized by clothing size, so you don't try to squeeze your toddler into the infant sleeper.

The remaining two-thirds of the closet is perfect to hold your clothes that are not in season, maternity clothes, or clothing that you are going to take to the thrift shop or Goodwill. I'm sure that you'll find use for this space. There's also the shelf on the top.

When David turns three, you may want to turn the closet into a space that's more accessible to his stature. If he's going to be asked to participate in straightening up his room, it helps if he can reach the rack. So, it's time to reorganize his closet.

The first step is:

1. Either lower the clothing pole that now exists to David's height, or add an additional pole at a level he can reach. The height of it should correspond to what his height will be for a year or two. He has the use of more than a third of the closet, but his space is now horizontal instead of vertical. The wheeled bins still work.

2. You may want to add shoe racks. Be creative. A few deep shelves attached to the back wall of the closet may be the perfect spot to house more toys.

If you play your cards right and if you remove the top shelf from the closet and move the initial clothing pole up, you'll still have room for a good number of your shorter hanging items. (For more details, please flip to Chapter 12).

When Colleen starts hitting the mark, and she seems to grow an inch a week, it will be time to reorganize the closet, again. Be sure to include Colleen in the process. It will be fun to collaborate on this project and may encourage preteen Colleen to hang up her clothes.

IN THE SAND CASTLES OF THEIR MINDS

The floor of a kid's room is covered with the projects and inventions of an active and creative mind. And that is something all of us want to encourage. Therefore, clutter and clutter removal has to be seen in a somewhat different light. How long should the castle sit in the middle of the room? How many days do we wait for tea party guests until we realize that they are not coming? When is Tommy coming back to finish the marathon Monopoly game?

Let's gather the troops, pull out our supplies, and begin. Our expectations for the amount of participation from our helpers vary from age to age and child to child. The key is to make this cooperative effort a pleasant

Congratulations! You've really done a nice job organizing the room so that it's kid friendly. The collaborative effort with the children gave them a real sense of ownership and a pride. So put on some music that has a good beat that you can all enjoy and dance your booties off!

The Lazy Way

experience for all concerned. The cleaning tools that you'll need are in the linen closet in the hall. The vacuum cleaner is in the broom closet in the kitchen.

- Bleaching cleanser
- Window or mirror spray
- An empty spray bottle for your cleaning assistant
- Paper towels
- Sponges
- Cotton swabs
- Toothpicks
- Plastic, drawstring garbage bags
- Carpet stain remover
- Electric vacuum cleaner for parent
- Non-motorized vacuum cleaner for cleaning assistant

Call for a Daily Pick-up

Do you remember my mentioning the KISS principle (Keep It Simple, Stupid) at the beginning of this chapter? It's so important to bear this in mind when you're trying to teach cooperation and include your children in this tidying up process. As you bring them into it, don't create frustration; encourage them. Praise can turn a half-a-glass exploit into a full-blown achievement. So repeat after me:

IF YOU'RE SO
INCLINED

If you have a second floor hall closet and are lucky enough to have the space, a real convenience and time saver is to have a second vacuum cleaner housed there.

I Promise to:

- Make things accessible for their height and capabilities.
- Ask them to perform only age-appropriate tasks.
- Show by example.
- Create a lasting (cleaned room) impression.
- Make it fun.

Even your toddler can help in the daily "pick-up-your-toys" routine. Here are some suggestions for making pick-up time as painless as possible:

1. Put on Daniel's favorite CD or tape and sing along with Barney or Raffi as you both return the toys to their proper slots. Try to choose a time before Danny gets over-tired and cranky. Otherwise, this parent/child experience will be brutal rather than bonding.

2. Make a game out of putting away dirty clothing. There are so many adorable laundry hampers on the market today. And they come in a variety of colors, patterns, and themes. I wouldn't be surprised if Michael Jordan's mother had him tossing his clothes into a bag designed like a basketball hoop when he was but a tyke.

3. Older children even can make a project out of designing their own laundry bags. You can purchase simple, inexpensive drawstring bags and, with a little fabric paint and glitter, turn them into works of

art. If Mom or Dad will assist with the glue gun, the decorating possibilities are endless. And Sara's pride and excitement about her invention will increase her desire to use it.

I Don't Want to Make My Bed!

I always found it a hassle and a frustration to change a simple crib sheet. It was exhausting having to remove the bumpers, unhook the crib toys from the railing, pull the crib away from the wall, fight with the contour sheet, which never seemed to fit after it was washed, replace the toys and bumpers, and finally push the crib back against the wall.

And this was before it was fashionable to use dust ruffles on cribs!

If I, as an adult, looked upon this task as a real pain in the neck, can you imagine how three-and-a-half-foot Christopher feels when he has to tackle a similar job with his new "big boy bed?" Yuck! No way. Get me out of here; I'd rather stay in diapers.

Don't frustrate him, KISS him:

1. Position the bed away from the wall, leaving Chris enough space to navigate.

2. Show him how to make one side of the bed completely and then make the other side. There is no need for little feet to run back and forth from the left side of the bed to the right side. That's no fun.

3. Choose simple bed linens. A fitted sheet, a top sheet, a pillow, and a quilt are enough for anyone to handle.

4. Let Chris choose which stuffed animals he wants to share his bed. If he just throws them on the bed instead of placing them in a pleasing pattern, who cares. At least they're not on the floor.

5. Forget the throw pillows; there's enough for little Chris to arrange.

6. And when Chris finishes the task and the quilt looks completely askew, hug him and compliment him on a great job.

When the Daily Pick-Up Just Won't Do It

The kids rooms really don't look that bad. Most of the toys are where they belong, except for Megan's operating table, which we promised could remain one more day until the liverwurst transplant has been completed. Little Michael (aka Beau) Jordan only missed one three pointer, a T-shirt in the corner, but very close to the laundry basket, I might add. Nice work. I see a major college scholarship in your future. The bins in the closet are working out very well. No one seems to mind putting his own clean laundry away. The twins, Stephanie and Seth, are finally able to keep their underwear straight. No more cross-dressing.

Let's survey the room to see if there have been any major mishaps we haven't heard about.

It looks like someone's been trying to copy the painting style of either Jackson Pollock or Georges Seurat onto the wall; it's hard to tell. Luckily, this artist used washable finger paints rather than oil. You can just squirt the wall

QUICK ⬛ PAINLESS

Let the kids sleep in their sleeping bag on top of the already made bed once a month, as a reward for a job well done. It will shorten your morning rush as well as theirs. They just have to roll up their bags and put them back where they're kept.

When removing a stain from any fabric or carpeting, be sure to test the material first in a small out-of-the-way spot that no one can see. Some fabrics are not colorfast. If you enthusiastically spray without testing, you may end up with a leopard-like look. Not the results you were looking for, and leopards are an endangered species.

with a spray cleaner and quickly wipe it up with a paper towel. Ask the painter to assist you in cleaning his canvas and add "easel" to your holiday shopping list.

For those few drops of paint that got onto the rug:

1. Use a clean white cloth or a paper towel when removing a spot with the aid of a stain remover. Otherwise, you take the risk of an accident waiting to happen. Not all fabrics are colorfast. You don't want to make matters worse by having the color of your cleaning cloth bleed onto the item from which you are trying to remove the mishap.

2. If the spill is fresh and still wet, hold a paper towel on the edge of the spill and try to draw as much of the liquid out of the rug as possible before you start blotting. Don't rub. Then, using a clean sponge, blot the stain with cold water and then blot again with a dry paper towel to absorb the liquid.

3. If the spill has dried, try blotting the stain with a clean wet sponge and then blotting, again, with a clean dry paper towel to absorb the liquid.

4. If this does not remove the paint entirely, let the carpet dry and then use a spot remover made for rugs. Follow the directions on the can. Remember, wipe the stain from the outside edge into the middle to keep the blemish contained in its original size and position.

Make way for the Clean Team. Sing along with me: Top to bottom, left to right, watch out Dust Bunnies, you're in for a fight. Let's start in the left front corner near the door and work our way around the room, ending up back where we started. First, let's check off what we've already done:

- Picked up the toys and put them back where they belong.

- Put all of the dirty clothes into the laundry hamper. Put the hamper in the hall so that it's ready to be taken to the laundry room.

- Put the dishes that were borrowed for the tea party into the picnic hamper near the staircase for the trip downstairs to the kitchen.

- Surveyed the room and eliminated any major stains and spills that needed extra attention.

Very good. It's time to move on to the next plateau. How long did it take you the last time you did a more thorough cleaning? Let's try to shave at least a minute off that time. Ready, set, go!

1. Put the extension on the static duster to clean those out of reach areas. Start at the ceiling and work your way down the wall, grabbing the dust particles and stubbing out the little cobwebs as you go. Let the kids take a turn. They'll love seeing how much higher they can reach since the last time they dusted.

2. Squirt a paper towel with window cleaner and gently wipe the pictures hanging on the wall. Don't forget the top of the frame that doesn't show. This hasn't been touched for a while.

IF YOU'RE SO
INCLINED

To keep your little helper motivated, post a list of all of the steps needed to clean the room. (If the room is fitted with a chalkboard or white board, you can even have the little one write a few down.) As you complete a step, have your child check it off, and both of you can cheer for your accomplishment.

3. The sports and academic trophies are next. A feather duster should do the trick. Pride alone has kept these shining.

4. As you pass the window, give it a spritz and a wipe wherever you see dirt or hand prints. Check the windowsill for dirt, dead bugs, or the ant collection that got away.

5. Dust the bedside lamp, clock, and tissue box holder.

6. Wipe off the tops of the night tables. Since this furniture is probably made of Formica or another washable material, a spray cleaner will easily handle that remnant of peanut butter cup that seems to have melted and gotten stuck way in the back corner and almost out of sight. (It might be a good idea to check under the bed before vacuuming.)

7. Be sure to check the fingerprints near the light switches. Wipe them off with the dampened paper towel. If someone was a bit heavy handed, a squirt with the spray cleaner will take them off.

8. Walk around the room, checking the corners and the rug for small pieces of toys that might accidentally get sucked up into the vacuum cleaner. Goodness knows, you don't want to devour Pocahontas.

9. Use the vacuum cleaner attachments to pick up the dirt on the moldings and baseboards.

QUICK n' PAINLESS

There are some tasks that children look forward to doing. And there are other assignments that they can just as well do without. Design a job wheel that you can tape onto the refrigerator. Turn the wheel and rotate the duties from child to child so that each one has the opportunity of participating in both pleasant and less than pleasant tasks.

10. Since you've kept the window treatment in this room fairly simple, you can skip vacuuming the valance this week. It looks fine.

11. This is the perfect day to change the linens. You take one side of the bed and Tyler takes the other side. Four hands are much faster than two no matter what the size.

12. Then grab your vacuum to pick up any lint on the rug. If you've decorated with low pile commercial carpeting, there will be no nap to deal with. If the vacuum is too heavy for Peter, let him use his Fisher-Price or Playskool model. Or if he's six or seven, the rechargeable electric broom may be his cleaning tool of choice. No matter what, share the job to demonstrate that it need not be a chore.

13. Don't forget those dust bunnies under the bed.

Finished! Pat yourselves on the back. Now what time did you say your neighbor was dropping off her three kids?

NINE, TEN, A BIG FAT HEN: HELPFUL HINTS

Bringing up kids, nowadays, is hard enough, and there are many times that we fly by the seat of our pants and make it up as we go along. I'll let you be creative in other areas, today. Here are a few helpful hints to save you time and energy and make your life move ahead a little smoother.

QUICK ⬭ PAINLESS

One of the best things I've found for picking up any liquid spill, even coffee, juices, and paint is a disposable diaper. They are designed to absorb, and do they. Once you've soaked up most of the mess, cleaning any residual stains is so much easier.

Low-Maintenance Merchandise

When you are in the process of setting up your child's room, here are a few brief and hopefully helpful hints that will make your life easier.

1. Low maintenance means:

   ▪ Washable

   ▪ Moveable

   ▪ Unbreakable

   ▪ Changeable

2. For sure footing, limit your carpet choices to:

   ▪ Low-pile commercial

   ▪ Heavy duty

   ▪ Practical color

   ▪ Scotch Garded in the factory

3. When it comes to walls, think:

   ▪ Washable paint

   ▪ Scrubbable wallpaper

And while you're thinking walls, why not add a few decorative touches to the kids' rooms that are OK to draw on? How about a chalkboard and lots of boxes of colored chalk? Or set up an easel? (Give the darlings berets and smocks but 86 any ideas of nude models.) Or you might want to get a little more dramatic by hanging a large, colorful wooden picture frame on the wall. (Painting the frame could be a project in itself. I would

A COMPLETE WASTE OF TIME

The Three Worst Carpets For a Child's Room:

1. **Thick plush that shows every movement, hides small objects from sight, and is not a flat foundation for creating a house of cards.**

2. **White, cream, or light beige in color. Need we say more?**

3. **One that can't take the abuse from automobile tires, furniture movers, painters, sculptors, and hamsters.**

do this in the basement, however.) Hang the chalkboard, or a flip chart of paper inside the frame. Then each piece that is painted is a framed work of art.

(If your kids really like to show their artistic talent, keep these easy clean-up canvases in mind: Finger painting in the bath while in the tub is a quick cleaner-upper. And right before it's going to rain, let the children decorate the driveway with driveway chalk.)

Also, hang a bulletin board on the wall, or turn a whole wall into a bulletin board, so that all the art work can be appropriately and professionally displayed. You might want to take this project one step further. Have the kids name their drawings and hang name tags next to the pieces as if they were hung in an art gallery.

YOU'LL THANK YOURSELF LATER

Buying the best quality washable paint will save you time and energy in the long run. And time is money.

Getting Time on Your Side

	The Old Way	**The Lazy Way**
Putting away toys	7 minutes	3 minutes
Making the bed	5 minutes	2 minutes
Picking up piles of dirty clothes	3 minutes	0 minutes
Hanging clothes in the closet	5 minutes	2 minutes
Washing the paint and crayons off the wall	10 minutes	3 minutes
Getting the kids to pitch in the clean-up	15 minutes (if you're lucky)	2 minutes

Behind Closed Doors: There's Never Enough Closet Space

Whether it's that first peek at your dorm room, shopping for your first apartment, or searching out the perfect retirement home, everyone scrutinizes the amount of closet space that's available. The dictionary definition of a clothes closet is "a small room for hanging clothes." Don't we all wish! In many cases, closets have to serve more than one master, so to speak. For example, if you remember Chapter 6, the hall closet, by necessity, stores the leaves to my dining room table.

GET A PLAN, STAN

The term "clean your closet" has a different connotation than "clean the kitchen." What you really mean is "have an orderly closet." Since there really isn't a lot of cleaning, like vacuuming and dusting, that can be done in a closet, cleaning

I like to choose a day when I'm "retaining fluid" (a day that I'm feeling fat, in other words) to clean out my closet. On those days, I have trouble using the excuse, "If I just loose a pound or two, the pants will fit." If you do the same, you'll probably get rid of a lot of old clothes.

a closet really means sorting through the junk and organizing efficiently.

Let's agree that, whether we like it or not, we will have assorted paraphernalia in our closets along with the clothing. Since you have limited space, you're going to have to face facts and eliminate some of the items you no longer use. Yup, you have to recycle them, give them away, or throw them out. We'll list some of the steps you can take here, and you'll find additional information in Chapter 5 on what to do with items that you no longer need.

Critique Your Clothes

If your closets are brimming over with clothes and you still have nothing to wear, it's time to take stock of what you own. You have to be objective. How would you respond to these statements? True or false?

- I haven't worn this item in the past two years.
- I got a lot of use out of it when it was an important part of my wardrobe.
- It was one of those things that I realized was a mistake after I bought it.
- I don't feel good when I wear it.
- It's no longer flattering.
- It no longer fits.
- It wouldn't be worth the money to take it to a dressmaker to have it redone.

Well, if you answered true to at least three of the above statements, may I suggest that you eliminate these items from your wardrobe? You'll not only make room in your closet, you'll be able to get a clearer picture of what you own and what you need. (I'll bet that you'll get rid of more than you hold on to. Once you start weeding out a few things here and there, you'll realize that you have certain outfits that are your favorites.)

What do you do with the clothing that you've decided to discard? Here are a few options:

1. Recycle it through a consignment store.

2. Donate it to a thrift shop, the Salvation Army, Goodwill, or another charitable organization of your choice.

3. Throw out those items that are of no use to anyone or that are in disrepair.

Is It a Memory or a Bad Dream?

If you are a saver, you'll have to fight the desire to keep it all. If and when you decide that some of it has to go, here are a few tips on what not to save:

1. If you think it's ugly, get rid of it, even if it is practical. You know you'll never use it unless you're home alone or there's a blackout.

2. It's time to toss the gift that you didn't like when you opened the box, but felt that you had to keep so as not to insult the giver.

QUICK 🔘 PAINLESS

Keep your closets as fresh as your rooms. Open the closet doors the next time you open your bedroom windows. The breeze will keep things smelling sweet and will air out some of the perfume and aftershave fragrances that cling to your clothing.

3. It's just plain broken—it's outta here. You know that you'll never get around to fixing it, and who would want to anyway?

4. Forget those "just in case" items: I'd better keep these three broken umbrellas just in case the four good ones that I own are being used or get lost.

If You Can't Even Give It Away. . .

Not everyone looks at your treasures through the same eyes as you do. For some, they may be just junk. Sorry. So if the consignment store doesn't want them, and there is not a charity in the world answering your request to donate them, then it's time to place them at the curb.

It's All in the Planning

The common element in most of your closets is the clothing. The other items are the extras that need a place to be stored. If you sort out your clothing first, it will give you a better handle on how much space is left for the rest of your stock. It's easy to decide which garments go into which closets; it's a little more difficult to determine where the most convenient place is to put the other stuff. Try this scheme:

1. Finish sorting your clothing for each individual closet.

2. Remove all of the extra merchandise and sort it according to kind:

   - China and serving pieces
   - Camera equipment

- Luggage
- Sports equipment
- Tablecloths and napkins
- Wrapping paper and bows
- Books
- And so on

3. Determine which is the most convenient closet for storing each of these non-clothing units.

4. Assess the kind of space that you'll need, and consider making some changes, such as:

- If your wardrobe consists of pieces that don't need much length when they are hung, (suits, jackets, skirts, shirts, and blouses) you might want to install double racks in your closet that will permit you to hang twice the amount of items in half the space.

- If you wear more dresses than suits, or if your attire is mostly casual, and you like to fold many articles, one rod and a series of bins and/or shelves may be the direction to take to solve your closet clutter.

5. Start organizing your closet. The trick is to expand the amount of space that seems to exist. Only you can decide what personal items you want to hold on to and which are ready to be discarded. Once you've bitten the bullet, you're on your way to uncluttering your closets. Create a picture in your mind that connects your lifestyle to your closet organization, and

IF YOU'RE SO
INCLINED

If you happen to know someone who would really like that gift that you don't particularly care for, why not give it to them? It may be "regifting," but you've solved some of your storage problems and made someone happy at the same time.

IF YOU'RE SO
INCLINED

If you're handy, you can purchase closet organizer kits at many home improvement stores. Shop around and get some ideas. Sketch out a plan on graph paper and you'll know just what to buy.

you may even enjoy choosing all the bells and whistles that go with an easier way of storing things and finding them when you need them.

6. Purchase the parts that you need to turn your closet into an efficient and well-organized area. One small suggestion, if I may. A project such as this is one best done with two pairs of hands.

7. Closet shops and do-it-yourself home stores carry a wide array of closet accessories that will keep your closet organized and put time on your side (no more frantically searching for the right tie and almost missing the 7:05 train). Some of these treasures are:

- Motorized tie racks

- Belt racks

- Hat racks

- Large hooks for hanging bathrobes

- Drawers that are lined with pacific cloth (this cloth inhibits tarnishing) and are divided into compartments to hold your jewelry

- Bins of every size and variety

- Drawers of all shapes and sizes

- Compartmentalized shelves onto which you empty your pockets at night

- Anything that you may need to have custom made

If you're not a "do-it-yourselfer" you may not be able to put this project into action without the aid of someone who knows the difference between a flat-head and a Philips screwdriver. It's okay to ask for assistance. You might call a professional organizer, someone who has a service in which they look at what you own and help you weed out the wheat from the chaff, so to speak. Then there are companies who do nothing but build organization into your closet space. Ask your friends, check the Yellow Pages in your local phone directory or read More Lazy Stuff: How to Get Someone Else to Do It (page 231).

CONTAIN AND MAINTAIN

The nice thing about the closet is that it rarely needs to be cleaned. Oh, you have to dust a little and throw out the non-essentials from time to time, but otherwise what's there to get dirty? The doors are closed. This is the perfect example of a closed container that hides any disorder and keeps out the dirt and grime.

Here are some tips for keeping your closets clean and orderly and your clothes neat.

Bust the Dust Bunnies

The premise used throughout this book is that a closed container prevents items from becoming dusty. And I did say that a closet is a closed container, and, therefore, you'd assume that a closet would be dust free. I wish that were true. But, in this case, we have to change "dust free" to "it won't collect a lot of dust." Here are a few ways that you can keep the dust to a minimum:

YOU'LL THANK YOURSELF LATER

If you've never executed a project like this before, ask someone to help you measure your closet area before you add organizers. Even if you are somewhat of an expert, it never hurts to have a second pair of eyes.

1. Try not to accumulate too many of your possessions on the floor. If you can keep this area as clear as possible, a quick swipe with an electric broom, vacuum or dust mop will do the trick. Even the dust bunnies won't be able to hide. (If you move into a new home, a closet cleaning seems to go along with the newness and a fresh paint job.)

2. Clothing that you do not wear often can sometimes pick up dust. Clear, heavy plastic zippered bags will keep them organized and dust free. The bags that have gussets (triangular inserts that enlarge the bag) on the sides will protect a greater number of outfits. (Two of the exceptions to storing in plastic are fur and suede. These materials need to breathe and would be better kept under wraps in cloth garment bags.)

3. Many cleaners cover the shoulders of freshly cleaned suits, dresses, and dry cleaned blouses with a piece of paper or tissue. If you leave this paper on the apparel, the shoulders will remain dust free. It's not pretty, but it works.

4. Have you noticed that in some dress stores, the darker clothes have plastic coverings that fit over the hook of the hanger and rest on the shoulders? It protects clothing from dust just as the paper from the dry cleaners does. You can use these covers over and over. It still isn't attractive, but it works.

5. You can leave the plastic dry cleaner's bags on out-fits that are delicate, dark in color, or not worn that often. This is really unattractive, but it works. (Tie the bottom of the bags so that they don't drag on the floor; it keeps your closet neater.)

These Shoes Are Made for Walking

Shoes scattered here and there can turn all of your closet organization topsy-turvy. Shoes placed in pairs are neat and tidy. Four ways to keep your feet together are:

1. Keep them in the boxes in which you purchased them. If you own a lot of shoes, keep them in the boxes that they came in. Most are labeled with the shoe color, and some even have a drawing of the shoe on the outside of the box. (If the box doesn't tell you what's inside, label it with a brief description of the shoe.) The boxes stack neatly, so it will be easy to find the pair that you're looking for.

2. Build a series of shoe bins into your closet organization scheme. It's offered as an option in many of the do-it-yourself kits.

3. Place shoe racks on the floor of your closet. Each shoe has its own holder on which to sit. The shoes do tend to get a little dusty, and you'll have to move the rack when you dust the floor.

4. There are shoe racks that hang over the back of a door. Some are metal and others are fabric or plastic. If you have a walk-in closet, you can hide

them on the side of the door that faces inside the closet. They are not made for a closet that has sliding doors.

Joan Crawford hated wire hangers. So do I. I know people who remove their freshly dry cleaned clothing from the wire hanger and transfer it to a wooden or padded one. I don't bother doing that; I just don't want to take the time. However, after I've worn something from the cleaners, I often change from the wire hanger it was on before I put it back in the closet.

- Padded hangers not only look attractive in your closet, they treat your more delicate clothing with additional care.

- Men's wooden suit hangers are designed to carry the weight of this style of clothing. The trousers hang over the cross bar and are held in place by a metal clasp. If you follow the pants' crease when you hang them up, they'll look pretty darned good when you put them back on.

- There are suit hangers made especially for suits that are worn by the "more athletically built" gentleman. They are replicas of regular-sized wooden suit hangers, but are constructed to hold the wider shoulder of the bigger suit. The shoulders of these larger sized suits are wider than the average sized wooden hangers and tend to droop and grow creases during the night. These hangers are a bit more expensive, but are worth the money.

QUICK ⬭ PAINLESS

Empty wire hangers dangling on a rod look messy. The next time you take your clothes to be cleaned, grab the wire hangers and take them with you. The dry cleaner will appreciate your recycling efforts.

Clip hangers snap onto the waistband of your skirts and also are terrific for hanging slacks. If you hang your trousers from the pant cuff rather than the waistband, it helps remove some wrinkles from the fabric.

A professional closet planner once told me that when you have double-hung rods, it's better to hang your wider clothing (such as jackets—the sleeves are wider than your other clothing) on the bottom pole, and the shirts, pants, and skirts on the top. For example, if this is the man's side of the closet, his suits and sports coats go on the bottom rack and his shirts go on the top. Not only does this keep the closet looking neater by keeping wider clothing below eye level, but it also increases the closet space by keeping the "skinnier" clothes on the top pole.

Bin There, Done That

The wire stackable bins that come in various sizes are terrific for organizing your closet, as well as sorting your laundry and saving you time. If you arrange one bin to hold your underwear, what's the point of folding it when it comes out of the dryer? Just toss it into the bin it belongs in. The wire also lets you know when you'd better start thinking about doing a load of laundry.

There's also a great time-saving trick for socks, but you're going to have to lay out some cash before you can use this one. Buy all new socks. Buy all the same style black socks, all the same style brown socks, and all the

A COMPLETE WASTE OF TIME

The Three Worst Uses for Wire Hangers

1. Drip drying clothing. They may leave rust stains.

2. Hanging men's wool three-piece suits. They cannot bear the weight.

3. Hanging a sweater. They leave funny impressions at the shoulders that look as though you are one of the original Trekkies.

same style blue socks. Designate a bin for each color sock. Now when you take them out of the dryer, you don't have to bother pairing them up; they're all the same. Just chuck the black into the black bin, the brown into the brown bin, and the blue into—you got it—the blue bin. When it's time to get dressed, simply grab two socks (from the same bin, of course).

This project was really kind of fun. There wasn't any heavy-duty cleaning at all. And if you play your cards right, there won't be for another 10 years. What are you going to do with all that empty closet space? You got it! Shop 'til you drop!

The Lazy Way

Getting Time on Your Side

	The Old Way	The Lazy Way
Looking for the other shoe	3 minutes	0 minutes
Pressing out wire hanger creases	3 minutes	0 minutes
Straightening up the closet	15 minutes	1 minute
Searching for your brown belt	5 minutes	0 minutes
Removing dust and lint from your black suit jacket	6 minutes	0 minutes
Finding the blouse that looks great with the skirt	15 minutes	1 minute

But They're Naturally Dirty: The Basement And Garage

You probably don't think much about cleaning these spaces since one is below the ground and the other is very close to the ground itself. But whether it's to straighten up the boxes of stuff we're saving or keep the cobwebs under control, there are times when these "dungeons" need our attention. It doesn't have to be torture though.

The Basement

For many, the basement holds the moments of your life: past, present, and future. This may sound a little sappy and corny, but if you think about it:

When you tire of your clothing, where do you put it until you get around to sorting it for Goodwill? Into the basement. When little Scott grows out of his clothes, where do you put them until they fit toddler Ira? Into the basement. When everyone is in a big girl or big boy bed, where do you store the crib? In the basement.

And the high chair? And the infant swing? And the outgrown car seats? Right. In the basement.

Where do you put your old kitchen table when you finally buy the butcher block one that you've been eyeing for months? Into the basement. (Since it is really too good to get rid of.) Where do you store the variety of tricycles, bicycles—three speeds, 10 speeds, and mountain bikes—until the next child in line grows into them? In the basement. Where to you keep the hot pink and green fake Tiffany lamp with the purple fringe on the shade that your spouse's parents gave you on your first anniversary? You know, the lamp that you take upstairs only when your in-laws are expected for their yearly month-long visit?

Need I say more?

CLOSE THE BARN DOOR! THE HORSE RAN AWAY

My washing machine sprung a leak today. Well, that's one way to clean the basement floor. Why does it take a disaster to get the basement organized? The only time that our cellar was perfectly straightened, had no extraneous material lying around, and was as clean as a whistle, was right after our entire neighborhood went through "the big flood." We had eight feet of water fill the basement. After the town had it pumped out, we employed a service that dealt only in disaster clean ups. They literally had to shovel out the debris. What a mess!

It took a month for the place to dry out, but once it did, it looked so gorgeous that I was tempted to call *Architectural Digest.*

Take Stock

Unfortunately, many of us don't take heed until catastrophe strikes. This incident taught me a few good lessons:

1. Periodically take stock of what's in the basement.

2. Make this inventory-taking time fun, yet mandatory, for each family member. No one can be responsible for the another person's treasures and memorabilia. And take it from one who knows, you never know when disaster will strike.

3. Try not to keep family photo albums, movies, and videos in the basement unless you absolutely have to. And even then, I suggest that you rethink your decision.

4. Don't store anything of value on the basement floor. Few households will have to live through a major flood, but many will experience:

   - The washing machine leaking.

   - The laundry tub over-flowing.

   - The sump pump breaking.

   - A power outage that shuts down the sump pump.

A COMPLETE WASTE OF TIME

The Three Worst Things to Store Near the Sump Pump

1. **Cartons filled with the children's elementary school mementos.**

2. **Cartons filled with your high school yearbooks.**

3. **The box with your grandmother's wedding dress.**

If you have children who are at an age when they like to play dress-up, save a few of your most ridiculous outfits and accessories for rainy days. Put them into a big wicker trunk or a big colored covered plastic storage bin. And the best place to keep the trunk or bin is at Grandma's house.

■ The tiny little constant trickle down the basement wall that seems to spread its tentacles further and further each time it rains.

■ General dampness, mold, and mildew.

Organize the Mishmash

Make this clean-up/inventory/organization, or whatever you want to call it, a group effort and a family affair. It will be fun to walk down memory lane together while you sort out the sports equipment. Replay all the Little League games and your days on the all-star team. Recall the ponytail league softball game when your daughter tripped over her own jersey while she was rounding second base, because she was so small and the shirt hung well below her knees. Talk about how your new athletic prowess has turned to golf and tennis. Share your handicaps (or not).

Follow the same pattern in organizing and sorting through your belongings that outlined in Chapter 12.

1. Recycle it through a consignment store.

2. Donate it to a thrift shop, the Salvation Army, Goodwill, or another charitable organization of your choice.

3. Throw out those items that are of no use to anyone or that are in disrepair.

Working as a family may help you adopt a more objective approach to what to save and what to give away. If your siblings teased you unmercifully 10 years ago when you wore that jacket, why continue to take the abuse? Dump it!

Shelve It

Okay. You've gone through the process of sorting the wheat from the chaff. And a job well done, I might add. I'll bet that after all the practice you've had in the preceding chapters, you've been able to cut a few minutes off your organization time. Was this your personal best?

There is an extra step that you really should take in the basement. When you are putting your possessions away, stockpile everything as far off the floor as possible. Even a little drip of water can be destructive. Here are a few suggestions for above the ground storage:

- Freestanding metal shelf units. They can be found in a variety of catalogs, do-it-yourself home stores, and large discount outlets and warehouses. Again, don't waste your money on flimsy merchandise. You're going to want these shelves to last for a long time; they need to be able to take the weight.

- Shelves that you can attach right to the wall studs. This type employs metal brackets that suspend the shelf. Since this is the basement, utility is the key, and you don't have to invest in a fancy bracket or decorator shelf. The brackets and shelves come in a variety of sizes and widths. Buy as heavy a bracket and as deep a shelf as you can. Many of the items that remain in the basement are big and bulky.

- Custom-built shelves that are about two feet deep. Attach them with two-by-fours and use press-board

YOU'LL THANK YOURSELF LATER

Do not store pictures, baseball cards, or other important paper mementos in the basement. Even a pin hole leak in a pipe can wash your memories away forever.

for the shelves themselves. They need not be painted; the raw wood looks just fine and suits the purpose. Position the bottom shelf at least a foot from the floor. This two-foot-deep shelf will hold a variety of objects from luggage to a major punch bowl to a good-sized carton. If you are able to leave two feet between each shelf there will be plenty of room to stack your boxes.

Individual shelves placed in strategic points around the basement:

1. Put a shelf near the washer and dryer to hold all of your laundry supplies.

2. Attach a few shelves in a corner of the basement for the extra cleaning supplies, garbage bags, paper towels, toilet paper, and tissues. (Your supply and shopping guides are in Chapters 1 and 3.)

3. A deep shelf or two are great for holding the turkey roaster and the extra large soup pot.

4. Designate a shelf or two for paint cans and painting supplies.

5. Don't forget the handyman of your house. Set aside a space to house all the equipment for those do-it-yourself projects. Be sure that you make the space large enough in the beginning; otherwise, it can spill over into other areas.

6. If you're a gardener, you may want to set up a potting table and a set of shelves to hold your clay pots,

potting soil, gardening tools, and bags of Spanish moss.

Box It

There are lots of items that you'll want to keep in closed containers, especially belongings that will probably never see the light of day again. If you choose to use cardboard boxes:

- Don't select sloppy seconds. Liquor stores still have pretty good boxes that they are willing to give away. The dividers come in handy if you are packing away glasses or other breakable items. Grocery stores tend to rip the tops off the boxes before they dump them. I, personally, would not choose a box in which vegetables were delivered. You never know what's been crawling around in them or what larva is ready to hatch.

- Try to find boxes that are similar in size and shape. It makes it easier and neater to stack them. Office supply houses, moving companies, and U-Haul dealers have terrific boxes they sell to their customers. They come in various sizes and have areas for labels on both the tops and the sides.

- House boxes on shelves or raise them above the floor, if only a few inches. The slightest trickle of water can soak into cardboard and form a soft spot that can later become mildew. A weak spot in the box will most likely tear if you ever decide to move it.

YOU'LL THANK YOURSELF LATER

Be specific when you label the content of the boxes. The more detailed you are, the easier it will be to find what you're looking for. All your neat packing and stacking can go for naught if David rifles through box after box looking for the fire hydrant costume from his first grade theater debut.

░ Buy boxes that are specifically made to store Christmas ornaments. They come decorated with a festive holiday design that makes them easy to spot. The inside compartments protect your ornaments from breakage.

There are a variety of heavy plastic containers on the market that come in various sizes and colors. Many are quite large. Some are opaque and others are clear so that you're able to see their contents. They have lids that fit securely on top. If your basement tends to be on the damp side, these bins will suit you to a tee. They stack well. You may even consider color coding your possessions for easier accessibility.

Hang It

A pegboard hung with hooks above the worktable and/or the potting table is a great organizing feature and a boon to the handyman (or maybe I should say handyperson). A hammer, screwdrivers, wrenches, a trowel, work gloves, and more dangle from individual pegs. All your tools are kept in sight. And if you remember to put them back on the hooks from which they were taken, they'll be there the next time you need them.

There are also some terrific clamp-type holders that you can buy in any hardware store that will suspend your brooms, mops, and dustpans and keep them orderly and off the floor. These clamps screw right into a two-by-four, which you can attach to a pair of studs.

Bag It

Large plastic drawstring garbage bags fit the bill for keeping snowsuits, hats, and scarves together during the months when they are not needed. After you have washed and dried them, toss them into the bag and set them on an empty shelf until Old Man Winter gives a nod. You could also rinse the salt from your boots and galoshes at the same time. Let them dry and put them into another garbage bag. Keep all of your winter outerwear together on the same shelf; you will eliminate that yearly frantic search at the first snowfall. Since all black garbage bags look alike, take an extra minute to stick labels on them listing what's inside.

Stack It

The basement is probably where you stash your lawn furniture in the off season. Hose the pieces off before you put them away for the winter. This furniture often can be cumbersome, but find an area of your basement that is devoted to outdoor items, and stack them all together. You may want to bag the cushions to keep them dust free for the next few months.

CLEANING THE CATACOMBS

Are you beginning to see a pattern here? In the past 12 chapters, you've: 1. categorized the clutter, 2. synthesized the surplus, 3. deleted the dreck, 4. flushed out the fluff, and 5. rewarded yourself for your efforts.

We're now down to #4 on our list for the basement. This really is a short and sweet process. You've done all

YOU'LL THANK YOURSELF LATER

At the same time you put away your lawn furniture for the winter, shut the water lines that lead to your outdoor faucets. Then open, and leave open, the faucets on the outside of the house so that they drain. Now you don't have to worry about these lines freezing and bursting during freezing weather and flooding the basement.

the major work already. One nice thing about having all of your storage items off the floor is that you can make a clean sweep of the room without having to move anything around.

Cleaning Down Under

I consider the actual basement-cleaning process to be only three steps, with an optional fourth:

You'll need:

- Angle broom
- Push broom
- Rags
- Feather duster
- Paper towels
- Window cleaner
- Bucket
- Mop
- Newspaper

1 **Dust the walls, pipes, and beams:** As with all of the other rooms in your house, start at the ceiling and work your way down. That way, any dirt that drops to the floor will get swept up in your final cleaning step. Let's drop those spider webs first. (Have you noticed that spiders seem to be the most fertile in the basement? I suggest throwing this garbage away outside, or those spiders might just get out of the trash and launch a counterattack.) Dust off the light bulbs, too. This is a good job for your feather duster.

QUICK n' PAINLESS

When cleaning the cobwebs, don't use your good feather duster. Just grab a really old rag, wrap it around the bristles of a broom, and dab at the webs until you get them down. Don't bother washing the rag; just throw it away when you're finished.

2 **Wash the windows:** You'll probably do this once, maybe twice a year. Or you may decide never to do it again, after this. You can hose the outsides of the basement windows the next time you water the lawn.

3 **Sweep the floor.** This is a good place to use the tip from Chapter 8. Put a sheet of newspaper on the floor. Wet the corners, slightly, to keep the paper in place. Use the newspaper as if it were a dustpan. Sweep the debris onto the paper. When you finish, roll the paper up and throw it into the garbage. Work your way around the basement, clubbing the spiders and sweeping in sections.

4 **Optional Step:** Wash the floor. If you decide that you want to do this, start uphill from the sump pump or drain and work your way down. Be sure that everything is up off the floor and that nothing lies in your path.

QUICK **n** *PAINLESS*

Next time you're in the yard with the hose, in addition to hosing off the basement windows, spray the overhang and the window wells.

A Breath of Fresh Air

To help relieve some of the stuffiness in the basement:

- Open the windows for an hour or two on a nice day.

- Put air fresheners around the room.

- Place small plastic cups, half filled with white vinegar, in strategic locations.

- Spray the room with white vinegar.

- Install a dehumidifier.

Hang a tennis ball on a string from the ceiling of your garage, so that the tennis ball hits the front windshield of your car when you reach your perfect parking spot. Now you won't smash into the wood piled on the back garage wall every time you park the car.

THE GARAGE

Do You Need a Giant Shoe Horn to Fit Your Car Into the Garage?

Do you find yourself parking on the driveway, or in the street, because there is no room in the garage for your car? This is a pretty expensive piece of machinery to let sit outside and face the elements. And, don't you just hate getting into a freezing cold car on a winter's morning or a sauna in the summer? Let's take stock of the situation, and get your Tin Lizzy back where it belongs.

Following our prescribed, tried and true pattern, let's:

Categorize the Clutter:

- Bicycles
- Seasoned wood for the fireplace
- Blue recycling bin required by the town for garbage pick-up
- One or two large covered garbage cans
- Two half bottles of windshield washer fluid
- Extremely large flower pots that you fill during the summer and place on the front porch and the deck
- A variety of boxes of food for shrubs, flowers, new growth, old growth, and tired growth
- Shovels, rakes, and an extensive variety of lawn equipment
- A 50-foot hose
- One mismatched lawn chair cushion

- A case of bottled water and a variety of soda pop
- Three lawn sprinklers (two broken)

The next step is to:

Synthesize the Surplus:

1. Hang your bicycles from the ceiling. Use large hooks, specifically designed for this purpose. It takes two hooks to suspend a single bike. Be sure that you screw the hooks into joists.

2. Stack the wood against the back wall of the garage. If you're not skilled in the art of the compact wood-piling, there are racks available that will prevent the logs from falling onto the floor. Depending upon size, these frames can hold a quarter, half, or full cord of wood.

3. Install shelves on the garage walls. Once again, be sure that you screw the brackets into the studs for the support that they'll need. (FYI, studs are placed 16 inches apart.) You might want to pinpoint one of the shelves to hold the boxes of plant and flower food. Use a second shelf for automobile supplies: the extra bottle of windshield washer fluid (consolidate the two half bottles) and ice scrapers. Include a deep shelf in your purchases on which to stack the large clay flowerpots, a bag of potting soil, and your gardening gloves.

4. Hang another pegboard, similar to the one that you used in the basement. This one will organize your

QUICK IN PAINLESS

Garbage can caddies on wheels will not only make your treck to the curb easier, it will keep the cans neatly placed against the wall where they belong.

QUICK *n* PAINLESS

Sit a doormat at the garage door that leads into the house so that you don't track oil, grease, and winter slush indoors.

gardening tools. Give yourself enough space for the push broom, rake, two shovels, a hoe, trowel, clippers, and so on. Stand larger, heavier tools, like a pick ax, on the floor with their handles facing up. Screw large hooks, almost the size of the ones that are holding up the bikes, into the wall, perpendicular to the floor. They will hold the handles of the tools in place and prevent them from falling over.

5. Keep the hose off the garage floor. Use a caddy to contain it when it's not in use. You may choose one that is wall-mounted or one that is freestanding. The latter comes with a set of wheels to help roll the hose from place to place.

6. Find a convenient spot near the door into the house for the recycling bin, the water, and soda.

7. During the summer, garage space may be at a premium due to the fertilizer spreader and lawn mower. These items can be moved down to the basement during the winter.

8. Be sure to check out catalogs and home improvement stores for other types of organizers that can resolve your unique needs.

Every family is different and so is the stuff stored inside your garage. If you utilize the general concepts of shelves, pegboards, hooks, and organizers you'll make your life a lot simpler and cleaning a lot easier.

Delete the Dreck

Don't debate it; toss it. Out go the broken flowerpots, broken lawn sprinklers, old smelly garbage can, and the mildewed cushion that fits on a chair that you no longer own.

Have a Hose-Down

It's time to clean up. Unfortunately, unlike the basement, the garage needs to be freshened up more than once a year. This dirt is more than just fluff. The spring cleanup is a little more involved because of all the slush, dirt, and gravel that has settled on the floor over the winter. It only takes a few steps to put the garage in order:

Pick It Up

1 If it has a hook or a peg to hang on, attach it.

2 Take everything that sits on the floor and set it outside.

Clean It Up

1 Wrap an old rag around the angle broom and attack the cobwebs.

2 Take the large push broom down from the pegboard and start pushing.

3 This is another great spot to employ the newspaper-on-the-floor-in-place-of-a-dustpan technique.

IF YOU'RE SO INCLINED

When it comes to a "looking spotless" trick, a coat of paint in the garage will brighten the place up and make it look a bit tidier. This is the room where you can let your creative juices flow. Be daring with your color scheme. Let the kids help out. What difference does it make if there are a few drips on the floor?

Wash It Out

1 Hose down the garage. Start in the back and aim the hose toward the driveway. The power of the spray will wash the dirt right down the driveway and into the street. You may need to use the push broom to help the water a little.

Put It Back

1 Let the garage floor dry before you put the items back that go on the floor.

Well, you're finished! You've done it. Every room in your house looks great. Congratulations for many jobs well done.

The basement and the garage were really dirty jobs, but ones that you won't have to repeat for quite a while. It's such a beautiful day. Why not pack a picnic and take off for the beach? You deserve it.

The Lazy Way

Getting Time on Your Side

	The Old Way	The Lazy Way
Remembering where you put the Philips screwdriver	3 minutes	0 minutes
Getting to the lawnmower	5 minutes	1 minute
Cleaning the garage	2 hours	30 minutes
Looking for the old high chair	10 minutes	1 minute
Finding the extra pin for the basketball pump	5 minutes	1 minute

More Lazy Stuff

How to Get Someone Else to Do It

Whether you've decided to give up all together, or just want to get some help once in a while, when it comes to hiring a cleaning service or individual, you'll want to make sure you're getting your money's worth, right? Otherwise, you'll find yourself cleaning up after you've just cut a check for 70 bucks. If you choose the right service, paying another person to complete the assignment is worth every penny you spend, as long as it makes you happy and your life easier. Here are places to go to find outside cleaning help, as well as some things to look for when choosing a service.

CALL IN THE TROOPS

If you so desire, you can hire someone to do almost anything that requires doing around your home. Here are just a few projects to hang your hat on:

- General housecleaning
- Carpet cleaning
- Furniture cleaning

- Drapery cleaning

- Window washing

- Cleaning out the garage

- Chimney cleaning

- Organizing the clutter

- Shopping for cleaning supplies

Who Do You Call?

Begin by putting together a list of names of professionals.

1. Ask your friends for names of companies that they have used and with whom they have been satisfied.

2. Search the Yellow Pages of your local phone book. The headings that you need to look under are:

   - Carpet Cleaners

   - Drapery and Curtain Cleaners

   - Furniture Cleaning Services

   - Cleaners—Industrial and Residential

   - Chimney Cleaners

   - House Cleaning Services

   - Maids: Merry Maids and Penny Brite Household Services, nationally

3. Check out the coupons that come in the mail, such as in Super Coups and ValUPack envelopes, for advertised cleaning services. (They'll also offer a discount.)

4. Read the flyers that get attached to your front door or mailbox.

Number one on this list is your best route. You know what your friends expect when they hire someone to do a job for them; a satisfied customer is the best reference that a business can have. No matter how you choose to search for the right professional, there are still a few steps that you should take along the way:

- Interview: Have each company come out to your home so that you can meet the people and show them exactly what the job is that you want done. Neither of you wants any surprises.

- Don't take the first offer: Talk to more than one company and get a quote from each.

- Get it in writing: Have the service put the quote in writing along with a description of the job that they are going to perform for you. Many businesses will guarantee the price for 30 days.

- Ask for references.

- Ask if they are bonded.

- Ask for a copy of their liability insurance policy.

Any Other Tips?

There are just a few more suggestions:

- Don't hand out up-front money. A reputable company can afford to pay for the supplies they need to do the work. That's part of being in business.

- Don't give anyone with whom you have not worked for a long period of time access to your home when you are not there. Make an appointment for these various services to do the job when you can be around to supervise.

- For projects such as cleaning and painting the garage, try calling a temporary staffing service for their assistance. Be sure to ask them about their interview and reference process and whether or not they have a four-hour guarantee. (If the people they send do not work out within the first four hours on the job, the staffing service will replace them at no additional charge.) You have to be on hand to supervise the work.

HIRE SOMEONE TO ORGANIZE?

As you've noticed, the first step to cleaning, as well as a strategy to keeping the house clean, is organizing all of your stuff. If you can deal with the spritzing and sweeping, but not conquering the clutter, you may want to consider hiring someone else to put your belongings in order. Yes. Nowadays anything's possible for a price.

Closets: There are several firms that will organize your closets. They come to your home, assess your needs, design an organizational system, and install it in a day. All you have to do is remove everything from your closet and remove the fixtures that are there now. In the Yellow Pages they are listed under "Closet and Closet Accessories."

Other stuff: Organizing has become a new service business. It may not be available in your city, as yet, but check the Yellow Pages under "Organizing Services— Household and Business." You might also review your community newspapers; many small businesses find this paper a good environment in which to advertise.

No matter whom you hire to work around your home, keep in mind that you are the customer and your expectations should be met. On the other hand, be sure that you keep your end of the bargain. If you've contracted with a company to perform two tasks around your home and then you ask them to do five, their final bill will reflect five jobs. So that you won't be surprised and upset when they hand you the tab, ask the cost of each individual assignment before you tell the professional to go ahead.

Nothing can be more rewarding than being able to call on a reliable professional to get the job done. And done right the first time. That's the lazy way.

If You Really Want More, Read These

Just in case you've suddenly taken a liking to cleaning and find the desire to learn more about it, I've listed here some of the other titles you'll find on your bookstore shelves.

Clutter Free! Finally and Forever, Don Aslett (Marsh Creek Press, 1995).

Clutter's Last Stand, Don Aslett (Writer's Digest Books, 1984).

Is There Life After Housework? Don Aslett (Writer's Digest Books, 1992).

Too Busy To Clean? Patti Barrett (Storey Books, 1998).

Clutter Control, Jeff Campbell and The Clean Team (Dell Publishing, 1992).

Speed Cleaning, Jeff Campbell and The Clean Team (Dell Publishing, 1991).

Spring Cleaning, Jeff Campbell and The Clean Team (Dell Publishing, 1989).

Talking Dirt, Jeff Campbell and The Clean Team (Dell Publishing, 1997).

Simply Organized, Connie Cox and Chris Evatt (Perigee Books, 1988).

How To Conquer Clutter, Stephanie Culp (Writer's Digest Books, 1990).

Messie No More, Sandra Felton (Fleming H. Revell, 1989).

The Messie Manual, Sandra Felton (Fleming H. Revell, 1981).

It's Here . . . Somewhere, Alice Fulton and Pauline Hatch (Writer's Digest Books, 1991).

How To Avoid Housework, Paula Jhung (A Fireside Book, 1995).

Don't Be A Slave To Housework, Pam McClellan (Better Way Books, 1995).

Totally Organized The Bonnie McCullough Way, Bonnie McCullough (St. Martin's Press, 1980).

Woman's Day magazine

For you Web surfers, there's a sight that mainly focuses on how to save money, but often includes articles on cleaning tips. It's called "The Dollar Stretcher," hosted by Gary Foreman. The address is www.stretcher.com.

If You Don't Know What It Does, Look Here

For a real eye opener, walk down the aisles of your supermarket and check out the number of cleaning products that adorn the shelves. It's amazing! The merchandise listed below is what I found in my local grocery store. What's on your grocer's shelves may vary from these, but I'm sure that you'll be able to find exactly what you're looking for. (Please note that not all labels are carried in every section of the country; they are not carried by every supermarket; a new product line may not have hit the shelves in your store as yet, or the item might be sold out.) Why not try one or two in each cleaning category to see if you prefer one over another? I'm not endorsing any one product, but those that I have tried have an asterisk after the name.

The representations of the products are taken from what is illustrated on the label by the manufacturer. If there is a series of goods under one general tag, you will find the description under the first listing and the other variations of the product line cataloged underneath. (For example there are several categories of products under the Windex label.)

The entire description of each product is not listed here. In some cases, the manufacturer only used the nomenclature "All-Purpose Cleaner." Be sure to read all labels before you toss the item into your shopping cart. Check to see if you can safely use the cleaner on the surface for which you intend it. The manufacturers are quite specific.

ALL-PURPOSE CLEANERS: USED FOR GENERAL HOUSEHOLD CLEANING ON A VARIETY OF SURFACES.

409 Products:

- *409 Glass and Surface Cleaner:* Cleans windows and household surfaces. Cuts grease and grime; does not streak.
- *409 Pro:* anti-bacterial; for use on grease, grime, food stains, crayons, fingerprints.

Ammonia*: for general household cleaning; cleans and deodorizes; use on windows and mirrors; good for stripping wax floors; regular scent. Also available in lemon scent.

Dow Anti-Bacterial Disinfectant Cleaner: kills germs, deodorizes, and disinfects.

Fantastik*: cuts grease, cleans stains, soap scum, mold and mildew stains, cleans and sanitizes, lemon scented.

Grease Grizzly: indoor and outdoor cleaner good for grease, oil, grime, soil build-up; cleans concrete, brick, wood, aluminum, painted surfaces, outdoor grills.

Greased Lightning: spray cleaner and degreaser for fiberglass tubs, bathrooms, carpets.

Mr. Clean Products:

- *Mr. Clean All Purpose:* (concentrate); comes in regular, mountain falls, or lemon scented varieties.

- *Mr. Clean special care:* (concentrate) for delicate surfaces, hardwood, ceramic tile, brass, marble, newer no-wax floors.

- *Mr. Clean*: ammonia (concentrate).

Parson's Ammonia: for all washable surfaces; lemon scented.

Pine-Sol: liquid cleaner; cleans, disinfects, deodorizes, cuts grease, and deodorizes. Comes in lemon or "rain clean" scents.

Spic and Span: cleans all finished floors, countertops, cabinets, walls, fiberglass, appliances, toilets, and more. Available in concentrate, powder, or pine-scented varieties.

Sun and Earth: all natural, citrus scent, safe around children and pets, cuts grease safely, kitchen countertops, microwave ovens, lunch boxes, highchairs, and baby changing tables.

Top Job Products:

- *Top Job All-Purpose Cleaner:* for cleaning a variety of surfaces throughout the house. Also available in concentrate.

- *Top Job Special Care:* hardwood, ceramic tile, brass, marble ,and the newer no wax floors.
- *Top Job:* (ammonia)

Cleaners with Bleach

Clorox Clean-Up: gel and spray with bleach; contains powerful cleaners plus Clorox bleach; removes stains, grease, soap scum; has a fresh scent. Also comes in "rain scent."

Comet*: Multi-room liquid gel; cleans tough stains and soil; use on sinks, countertops, stove tops, tubs, tiles, no-wax floors, and toilet

Soft Scrub*: gently bleaches out tough stains on tubs, tile, sink, stovetops, toilets, and countertops. Use on greasy dirt, mildew stains, and soap scum.

BATHROOM CLEANERS

Shower Mold and Mildew Removers

Clean Shower Products:

- *Clean Shower* (original):* no chlorine, no bleach, no harsh fumes, no rinsing, wiping, scrubbing, squeegeeing; eliminates soap scum, hard-water deposits, and mildew stains. If you start with a clean shower, and use daily, you never have to clean your shower again. If you start with a dirty shower, use daily, it takes two to four weeks to have a completely clean shower.

- *Clean Shower (for acrylic, glass, and alcohol free):* Both Clean Shower products are made to last about four weeks. If streaking occurs, rinse off shower and use less Clean Shower.

Tilex Products:

- *Tilex Fresh Shower:* daily-use shower cleaner; no harsh chemicals; if you start with a clean shower and use daily, you'll never have to clean again; if you start with a dirty shower, it takes two to four weeks of daily use to have a clean shower. If there is streaking, rinse the shower and use less Tilex® Fresh Shower. The product was made to last about four weeks.

- *Tilex Mildew Cleaner*:* disinfects and kills mildew on hard non-porous surfaces.

- *Tilex Soap Scum Remover*:* cuts through tough soap scum, cleans and deodorizes bathroom surfaces, shower doors, and plastic surfaces. Do not use on marble, brass, or natural wood.

X-14: soap scum remover; spray, cleans dirt and hard water spots.

Toilet Bowl Cleaners

2000 Flushes Products:

- *2000 Flushes (with bleach):* tablets that you put into tank; they are concentrated to last for four months; bleaches away stains, safe for plumbing and septic systems.

- *2000 Flushes (blue and bleach)*: "blue freshness" plus chlorine bleach.

Clorox Products:

- *Clorox Toilet Bowl Cleaner*:* removes stains without bleach, deodorizes, and leaves the bowl sanitary; fresh scent.

- *Clorox Toilet Bowl Cleaner with Bleach*:* bleaching action, "rain" scent.

- *Clorox Bleach and Blue:* cleans and deodorizes when you flush; tablets last up to four months; leaves bowl sanitary and even cleans under the rim. Safe. Should be used in toilets that are flushed daily.

- *Clorox Automatic:* sanitizing, without bluing; tablets that go into tank; kills germs, cleans, deodorizes after each flush; each tablet sanitizes for seven weeks.

Lime-Away*: dissolves lime, calcium, and rust stains as well as hard water build-up; leaves toilets clean and fresh smelling.

Lysol Toilet Bowl Cleaner* (with bleach): thick liquid coats and bleaches the bowl. For cleaning and deodorizing. Also available in non-bleach formula.

Ty-D-Bol Products:

- *Ty-D-Bol:* a tablet that is safe for plumbing and septic tank systems; cleans with every flush; floral scent.

- *Ty-D-Bol:* concentrated, time-released formula that is safe to use with bleaches or cleansers; phosphate free; blue spruce scent.

Vanish Products:

- *Vanish Automatic*:* pour into tank; continuously acts against stains, odors, and dirt build-up.
- *Vanish Drop-Ins:* contains bleach; repels tough stains from hard water, minerals, and lime scale.
- *Vanish Hang-Ins:* hang inside tank; cleans up to four months; uniquely designed dispenser.

Counter, Tile, and Basin Cleaners

Comet: heavy duty, cleans tough bathroom soils and hard water stains, non-abrasive, no bleach.

Dow Bathroom Cleaner*: disinfects, cleans, and shines without scratching; designed to attack soap scum and hard water stains. (Dow lists a line of cleaning products designed for almost any cleaning purpose.)

Dow Bathroom Cleaner for Soap Scum and Mildew: a stain remover with "scrubbing bubbles."

Lysol Products:

- *Lysol Basin, Tub & Tile Cleaner*:* cleans, shines, and disinfects washable bathroom surfaces and fixtures; has a dual nozzle that pulls out for foam and pushes in for spray.
- *Lysol Cling:* a thick liquid toilet bowl cleaner, country scent, deodorizes, and disinfects.
- *Lysol Foaming Spray:* same as above, but in an aerosol container.

Scrub Free: soap scum remover, works on contact, lemon scent, no scrubbing, and no scratching.

CARPET CLEANERS

409 Spray: Removes grease, dirt and odors; spray, dry for 15 minutes, and then vacuum.

Carbona: carpet and upholstery cleaner, comes with a sponge/brush applicator, for heavy-duty carpet cleaning.

Resolve Products:

- *Resolve* (regular)*:* cleans all stains, even spaghetti sauce.
- Resolve (high traffic): comes with a full-size scrub brush like the ones your grandmother used to clean her kitchen floor; safe on wool, nylon, and stain resistant carpets.

Woolite Products: an array of carpet cleaning products in foams and sprays.

- *Woolite:* for heavy traffic areas.
- *Woolite*:* one step, spray or squirt the cleaner on the stain, let it work a few minutes and then vacuum.
- *Woolite:* for pet stains and odors; carpet and upholstery cleaner
- *Woolite Special Formulas:* Two sprays: (1) oil and grease stains, such as salad dressing, glue, spaghetti sauce; (2) protein and liquid stains, such as fruit juice, milk, coffee, pet urine.

DISHES

Dishwashing Liquid

Dawn Products: targeted grease cutter concentrates.

- Anti-bacterial
- Special Care
- Ultra: blue, original liquid; effective on grease.
- Ultra: same as above, but green, with "mountain spring" scent
- Ultra Lemon: yellow liquid

Dove*: cleans dishes, hand washables, countertops, and other surfaces, gives you soft hands.

Ivory*: grease cleaner, long-lasting suds.

Joy: cleans grease and grime off dishes. Available in anti-bacterial formula, as well as regular and lemon scented.

Palmolive Products: a variety of specialized dishwashing products; all are concentrates made to last longer with a specifically designed cap that regulates the amount of soap that squeezes out of the plastic bottle.

- Palmolive: original and lemon-lime scent.
- Palmolive: for sensitive skin.
- Palmolive: for pots and pans.
- Palmolive: antibacterial.

Sun Light*: lemon scent, cleans tough stains on dishes, also for fine washables; antibacterial hand soap.

Dishwasher Detergents

Cascade*: cleans dishes "virtually spotless," has "sheeting action." Available as powder or gel in regular or lemon scent.

Electrasol Products:

- *Electrasol*:* gel, with baking soda; dissolves quickly and gets dishes "sparkling clean"; lemon scent.
- *Electrasol:* tabs (unwrap the tab and put it into the soap dispenser).

Palmolive: gel, with built-in rinse aids, lemon scent. Also available with baking soda.

Sun Light: powder or gel, lemon scent, removes tough foods easily.

Dishwasher Rinse Aids

These products help to prevent water spots.

Cascade*: liquid, pour into dispenser in dishwasher; provides extra boost of sheeting action with rinse cycle. Check when to replace, usually once a month.

Jet Dry Products:

- *Jet Dry*:* regular; liquid, pours into dispenser in dishwasher, spot and residue fighter. Also comes in lemon scent.
- *Jet Dry:* dispenser hangs on top shelf of dishwasher, lemon scent.

FLOOR CLEANERS

Murphy Oil Soap*: household cleaner, for wood furniture, cabinets, floors (wood and no-wax), ceramic tile, painted surfaces, leather and vinyl; no dulling residue.

Pine Sol*: See All-Purpose Cleaners.

Spic and Span*: See All-Purpose Cleaners.

FURNITURE POLISH

Behold: cleans gently, shines, preserves, and protects; lemon scent.

Cabinet Magic Products:

- *Cabinet Magic:* for Formica and other laminates; spray.

- *Cabinet Magic:* for wood; spray.

Endust: cleans and dusts; no-wax dusting spray.

Guardsman: cleans, restores and protects, wax free, wood scent.

Life O' Wood*: restores the luster of varnished, lacquered, and enameled surfaces. Cleans and polishes wood.

Murphy Oil Soap*: See Floor Cleaners

Old English Products:

- *Old English:* wood polish, spray or oil; country scent.

- *Old English:* wood treatment, oil that comes in a bottle and is applied with a cloth; moisturizes and protects wood; lemon scent.

- *Old English*:* scratch cover; oil that comes in a bottle and is applied with a cloth; made for both lighter and darker woods.

Pledge Products*: all products are smear-free and restore the "natural beauty every time you dust." Sprays and pumps are available.

- *Pledge*:* in lemon, "country woods," "country garden," and "spruce fresh" scents.
- *Pledge:* combined formula for use on both glass and wood. (For example, a wood dresser with a glass top or a wood armoire with glass doors.)

KITCHEN PRODUCTS

Lysol Antibacterial Kitchen: cleans and disinfects washable nonporous kitchen surfaces, cuts grease, kills germs, citrus scent, spray and concentrate.

Dow Antibacterial Multi Purpose Cleaner: for the entire house.

See All Purpose Cleaners

See Powdered Cleansers

Appliances

See All Purpose Cleaners

See Cleaners with Bleach

See products listed under Kitchen Products

See Powdered Cleansers

Countertops

See All Purpose Cleaners

See Cleaners with Bleach

See products listed under Kitchen Products

See Powdered Cleansers

Brillo*: steel wool soap pads, for tough cleaning; shines.

Scotch Brite*: wool soap pads, never rust.

SOS*: steel wool soap pads; good for baked-on food and grease; shines pots and pans; cleans the stove, broiler, outdoor grill, rust stains.

Oven Cleaners

Easy-Off Products:

- *Easy-Off:* original, heavy duty; uses a warm oven or a cool oven overnight.

- *Easy-Off Fume Free Max:* penetrates grease and cleans with no fumes and no lye. Requires no heat; cleans in cold oven; lemon scent.

GLASS AND WINDOW CLEANERS

Windex Products: glass and window cleaner; cuts grease without streaking.

- *Windex*:* original, contains Ammonia D. Also available in potpourri scent.

- *Windex:* No drip.

- *Windex:* outdoor spray; attaches to your hose; spray will reach the second floor and will clean 18 to 23 windows; rinse the windows by switching the built-in dial to "rinse."
- *Windex:* professional; for glass surfaces and more. Cuts tough grease and grime. Streak-free shine; Ammonia D.
- *Windex:* with vinegar.

MISCELLANEOUS PRODUCTS

CLR*: removes calcium, lime, and rust deposits. Can use on tea and coffeepots, tubs, toilets and sinks, chrome and metal.

CLR Outdoor Furniture Cleaner: cleans plastic, rattan, wicker, wood, wrought iron, vinyl, PVC, and canvas; biodegradable.

Damp Check: moisture absorber; prevents mildew and odors.

Dispos'l Clean: for garbage disposals and sink drains; kills bacteria, including *salmonella choleraesuis.*

Iron Out: rust stain remover for toilets, sinks, dish washers, white clothes.

Powdered Cleansers

Cleaning powders for tubs, sinks, pots, and pans.

Bon Ami : "Hasn't scratched yet. If you need a little muscle and want a soft touch"; doesn't scratch hard surfaces. Safe for fiberglass.

Comet*: original green can; cleaning powders for tubs, sinks, pots, and pans. Also available in lemon scent (yellow can).

UPHOLSTERY CLEANERS

Carbona: See Carpet Cleaners.

Resolve: cleans fabric and upholstery.

Scotch Gard: spray fabric and upholstery cleaner; gently cleans and protects; leaves behind Scotch Gard fabric protection; restores fresh new look to colorfast household fabrics.

Woolite: Fabric and Upholstery Cleaner.

OTHER HOUSEHOLD TERMS

Formica: trademarked brand name for a laminate.

Generic Products: Not under a trademark; many times bearing the name of the supermarket.

Laminate: Material composed of layers of firmly united material, bonded with resin and compressed under heat. Used for kitchen counters and some furniture.

Linoleum: A durable, washable material made in sheets used as a floor covering.

Lucite: A trademarked term for an acrylic resin or plastic.

Nap: A soft, fuzzy fibrous surface usually raised by brushing against a rough surface.

Patina: A surface appearance (as a coloring or mellowing) of something that has grown beautiful, especially with age.

Pile: A mass of raised loops or tufts covering all or part of a fabric or carpet that is formed by extra warp or welt yarns during weaving, producing a soft velvety surface.

Veneer: A layer of wood of superior value or excellent grain for overlaying an inferior wood, usually by gluing.

It's Time for Your Reward

Once You've Done This	**Treat Yourself to This**
Organized the cleaning products throughout your home.	Rent that mushy romance movie you've been dying to see. Add a bag of microwave popcorn. Sheer heaven.
Taken your vacuum cleaner in to your friendly vacuum cleaner store for it's yearly check-up.	Stop by that antique shop that you've been eyeing to browse (or buy!).
Visited the discount warehouse and stocked your larder with a good four month's supply of cleaning products.	Relax your muscles with a long hot shower. Feeling the water pelt on your back would be great.
Taken your third, and last, trip to the consignment shop in the past 48 hours.	Have you ever had a triple dip ice cream cone? Me neither. Now's your chance!
Gathered all the loose photos that were stored in various places around the house and put them into one nice big hatbox.	Pour yourself a cup of coffee, put your feet up, and reminisce over the old family photos that you recently discovered. You know, the ones in which you had a full head of hair.

Once You've Done This	**Treat Yourself to This**
Work as a family to pair up the array of mismatched mittens and displaced scarves.	Go on a family celebration outing. Don those mittens and scarves and head for the skating rink!
You've plumped up your final cushion and tossed all of the throw pillows, being careful to cover-up the Spaghetti O's stain.	It's your turn for some private time. Curl up in your own private space. If a big bubble bath is what you crave, bring out the scented candles and crack open a bottle of champagne.
You bit the bullet and cleaned the oven and the refrigerator. And both on the same day, too!	After all this exercise you want a two-hour workout at the gym! Well, it's your choice. Be my guest.
You've assisted the twins in cleaning their bedroom.	Take a nap.
You've sorted and organized your closets. How spacious they are!	Shop 'til you drop!
You gave the garage a good hose down for its annual summer cleaning.	Pack a picnic and spend the rest of the day at the beach.

Where to Find What You're Looking For

Now you can do these tasks, too!

The Lazy Way™

Starting to think there are a few more of life's little tasks that you've been putting off? Don't worry—we've got you covered. Take a look at all of *The Lazy Way* books available. Just imagine—you can do almost anything *The Lazy Way!*

Cook Your Meals The Lazy Way
By Sharon Bowers
0-02-862644-3

Handle Your Money The Lazy Way
By Sarah Young Fisher and Carol Turkington
0-02-862632-X

Care for Your Home The Lazy Way
By Terry Meany
0-02-862646-X

Train Your Dog The Lazy Way
By Andrea Arden
0-87605180-8

Take Care of Your Car The Lazy Way
By Michael Kennedy and Carol Turkington
0-02-862647-8

Learn Spanish The Lazy Way
By Vivian Isaak and Bogumila Michalewicz
0-02-862650-8

*All Lazy Way books are just $12.95!

additional titles on the back!

Build Your Financial Future The Lazy Way
By Terry Meany
0-02-862648-6

Shed Some Pounds The Lazy Way
By Annette Cain and Becky Cortopassi-Carlson
0-02-862999-X

Organize Your Stuff The Lazy Way
By Toni Ahlgren
0-02-863000-9

Feed Your Kids Right The Lazy Way
By Virginia Van Vynckt
0-02-863001-7

Cut Your Spending The Lazy Way
By Leslie Haggin
0-02-863002-5

Stop Aging The Lazy Way
By Judy Myers, Ph.D.
0-02-862793-8

Get in Shape The Lazy Way
By Annette Cain
0-02-863010-6

Learn French The Lazy Way
By Christophe Desmaison
0-02-863011-4

Learn Italian The Lazy Way
By Gabrielle Euvino
0-02-863014-9

Keep Your Kids Busy The Lazy Way
By Barbara Nielsen and Patrick Wallace
0-02-863013-0